Trial Advocacy

Assignments and Case Files

ASPEN PUBLISHERS

Trial Advocacy
Assignments and Case Files

Marilyn J. Berger
Professor of Law
Seattle University School of Law

John B. Mitchell
Professor of Law
Seattle University School of Law

Ronald H. Clark
Distinguished Practitioner in Residence
Seattle University School of Law

Wolters Kluwer
Law & Business

AUSTIN   BOSTON   CHICAGO   NEW YORK   THE NETHERLANDS

© 2008 Marilyn J. Berger, John B. Mitchell, and Ronald H. Clark.
Published by Aspen Publishers. All Rights Reserved.

Aspen Publishers
Attn: Permissions Department
76 Ninth Avenue, 7th Floor
New York, NY   10011-5201

To contact Customer Care, e-mail customer.care@aspenpublishers.com,
call 1-800-234-1660, fax 1-800-901-9075, or mail correspondence to:

Aspen Publishers
Attn: Order Department
PO Box 990
Frederick, MD 21705

Printed in the United States of America.

1 2 3 4 5 6 7 8 9 0

ISBN 978-0-7355-7835-7

The Library of Congress has already cataloged the main work as follows:

Berger, Marilyn J.
  Trial advocacy : planning, analysis, and strategy / Marilyn J. Berger, John B.
Mitchell, Ronald H. Clark. — 2nd ed.
       p. cm.
  Includes index.
  ISBN 978-0-7355-7144-0 (pbk. : alk. paper) 1. Trial practice—United States.
I. Mitchell, John B. (John Barry), 1944- II. Clark, Ronald H. III. Title.

  KF8915.B45 2008
  347.73'7—dc22
                                                                    2008025580

ABOUT WOLTERS KLUWER LAW & BUSINESS

Wolters Kluwer Law & Business is a leading provider of research information and workflow solutions in key specialty areas. The strengths of the individual brands of Aspen Publishers, CCH, Kluwer Law International and Loislaw are aligned within Wolters Kluwer Law & Business to provide comprehensive, in-depth solutions and expert-authored content for the legal, professional and education markets.

CCH was founded in 1913 and has served more than four generations of business professionals and their clients. The CCH products in the Wolters Kluwer Law & Business group are highly regarded electronic and print resources for legal, securities, antitrust and trade regulation, government contracting, banking, pension, payroll, employment and labor, and healthcare reimbursement and compliance professionals.

Aspen Publishers is a leading information provider for attorneys, business professionals and law students. Written by preeminent authorities, Aspen products offer analytical and practical information in a range of specialty practice areas from securities law and intellectual property to mergers and acquisitions and pension/benefits. Aspen's trusted legal education resources provide professors and students with high-quality, up-to-date and effective resources for successful instruction and study in all areas of the law.

Kluwer Law International supplies the global business community with comprehensive English-language international legal information. Legal practitioners, corporate counsel and business executives around the world rely on the Kluwer Law International journals, loose-leafs, books and electronic products for authoritative information in many areas of international legal practice.

Loislaw is a premier provider of digitized legal content to small law firm practitioners of various specializations. Loislaw provides attorneys with the ability to quickly and efficiently find the necessary legal information they need, when and where they need it, by facilitating access to primary law as well as state-specific law, records, forms and treatises.

Wolters Kluwer Law & Business, a unit of Wolters Kluwer, is headquartered in New York and Riverwoods, Illinois. Wolters Kluwer is a leading multinational publisher and information services company.

Over the years, we have dedicated three books to our families. In that time, our children have grown, grandchildren have come into the world, and people around us have begun carrying their record players, televisions, and movie theaters in their telephones. So much change; but one thing has remained constant. Our families always are there for us. To now dedicate another book to them makes as much sense to us as dedicating our dinners, our walks, our evenings, or our vacations. They are part of everything; they are devoted to us, and we to them. This then is not a dedication; it is a gesture of our devotion.

To Albert J. and Dorian S.
Marilyn J. Berger

To Eva, David, Sarah, J.P., and Tyler—my family.
John B. Mitchell

To Nancy, Brady, Soojin, Malachi, Riley, Clancy, Kara, Colby, and Darren.
Ronald H. Clark

And to Laurie Sleeper, our administrative assistant, and her family.

What should we say about Laurie Sleeper, administrative assistant? She is not family, but watching her hover over us you might not know it. She has kept us going, kept us laughing, kept us organized, kept us on schedule, figured out the technology, and to the best of her considerable abilities has kept us relatively sane.

Summary of Contents

Contents..xi
Acknowledgments xix

Chapter One: Introduction to the Books, CDs, DVD, and Web Site..............1
Chapter Two: Trial Preparation and Case Management............................ 11
Chapter Three: The Assignments 1-84...59

Appendix A: Checklists for Trial Skills..183
Appendix B: Trial Case File Table of Contents 211

Contents

Acknowledgments xix

Chapter 1: Introduction to the Books, CDs, DVD, and Web Site 1

   I.   Introduction.. 1
      A. Overview 1
      B. The Books.. 1
      C. Icons and Boxes... 2
  II.   The CDs.. 3
      A. Case Files 3
      B. The Actors' Guide.. 3
  III. The DVD: Movie of a Trial and the Scene of the Crime................. 4
  IV. Web Site 4
   V. Rules of the Game 4
      A. Jurisdiction 4
      B. Evidence, Procedural, and Professional Responsibility
          Rules.. 5
      C. Dates 5
      D. Civil Case.. 5
      E. Your Responsibilities.. 6
      F. The Game 7
  VI. Factual Summary: *State v. Hard* and *Summers v. Hard*.................... 7

Chapter 2: Trial Preparation and Case Management 11

   I.   Introduction.. 11
  II.   Planning Case Development 12
      A. Case Theory as a Guide.. 12
      B. Researching Legal Theories.. 14
      C. Organizing the Fact Investigation..................................... 16
      D. Avoiding Tunnel Vision 18
      E. Focus Groups—Testing the Facts 19
      F. Resource Factors.. 19
      G. Informal and Formal Fact Investigation.............................. 20

III. Progression of a Case 24
    A. A Civil Case.. 24
    B. A Criminal Case 26
IV. Informal Fact Investigation 29
    A. The Investigator.. 29
    B. The Expert: Consultant and Witness..................... 29
    C. Should You Retain an Expert? 33
    D. Selecting an Expert.. 34
        1. Conclusions Compatible with Your Case Theory 34
        2. Skills of the Expert... 37
        3. Practical Problems 40
    E. Exhibits 42
V. Managing the Case 42
    A. Electronic Case Management................................ 43
    B. Trial System 46
VI. Ethical Considerations in Case Development and
Management 56
    A. Supervising the Investigation 56
    B. The Expert.. 56

Chapter 3: The Assignments 1-84 59

Table of Contents for the Assignments................................ 59

Chapters 1 and 2.   Today's Trial Lawyer and Trial Persuasion
                         Principles
   Criminal and Civil Case Assignments
    Assignment 1: The Role of a Trial Attorney in the
                      Adversary System............................... 67

Chapter 3. Case Theory and Theme Development
   Criminal and Civil Case Assignments
    Assignment 2: Prosecutor: Case Theory and Theme
                      Development
                      (Planning with the Aid of Closing Argument)......... 68
    Assignment 3: Defense Attorney: Case Theory and
                      Theme Development
                      (Planning with the Aid of Closing Argument)......... 69
    Assignment 4: Prosecutor and Defense Attorney:
                      Case Fact Development...................... 71
    Assignment 5: Prosecutor and Defense Attorney: Using
                      Case Analysis and Management Software 72
    Assignment 6: Prosecutor and Defense Counsel: Trial
                      Preparation
                      (Witnesses, Exhibits, Trial System) 73

Civil Case Assignments

Assignment 7: Plaintiffs' Attorney: Case Theory and
Theme Development
(Planning with the Aid of Closing Argument).........74

Assignment 8: Attorneys for Defendants Hard and Davola:
Case Theory and Theme Development
(Planning with the Aid of Closing Argument).........76

Assignment 9: Plaintiffs' and Defendants' Attorneys:
Case Fact Development.....................................78

Assignment 10: Plaintiffs' and Defendants' Attorneys:
Using Case Analysis and Management
Software...79

Assignment 11: Plaintiffs' Attorney and Attorneys for
Defendants Hard and Davola:
Trial Preparation
(Witnesses, Exhibits, Trial System) 80

Chapter 4. Trial Motion Advocacy

Criminal Case Assignments

Assignment 12: Prosecutor and Defense Attorney:
Planning Motions in Limine 81

Assignment 13: Prosecutor and Defense Attorney:
Prosecutor's Motion in Limine and
Defense Response
(Bruno Summers's Neo-Nazi Activities) 83

Assignment 14: Defense Attorney and Prosecutor:
Defense Motion in Limine and
Prosecutor Response
(Photographs)...85

Civil Case Assignments

Assignment 15: Plaintiffs' and Defendants' Attorneys:
Planning Motions in Limine 86

Assignment 16: Attorneys for Defendant Davola and
Plaintiffs: Defense Motion in Limine and
Plaintiffs' Response
(Exclusion of Psychiatric Opinion)......................88

Chapter 5. Making and Meeting Objections

Criminal and Civil Case Assignments

Assignment 17: Attorneys for Defendants Hard and Davola:
Making and Responding to Objections
(Peter Dean) 90

Chapter 6. Jury Selection: Two-Way Exchange
Criminal Case Assignments
   Assignment 18: Prosecutor and Defense Attorney:
                  Conducting Jury Selection 92
Civil Case Assignments
   Assignment 19: Plaintiffs' and Defendants' Attorneys:
                  Conducting Jury Selection 93

Chapter 7. Opening Statement: Storytelling
Criminal and Civil Case Assignments
   Assignment 20: Prosecutor and Plaintiffs' Attorney:
                  Planning an Opening Statement......................... 95
   Assignment 21: Defendants' Attorneys: Planning an
                  Opening Statement 97
   Assignment 22: Prosecutor, Plaintiffs', and Defendants'
                  Attorneys: Deliver an Opening Statement........... 98

Chapter 8. Exhibits and the Visual Trial
Criminal and Civil Case Assignments
   Assignment 23: Prosecutor and Plaintiffs' Attorney: Videotape
                  of the Garage Tavern and Scene Visit
                  (Detective Tharp)... 99
   Assignment 24: Prosecutor and Plaintiffs' Attorney:
                  Scale Diagrams of the Garage Tavern
                  (John Lacey, Peter Nye)...................................... 100
   Assignment 25: Prosecutor and Plaintiffs' Attorney:
                  Photographs of the Garage Tavern
                  (Detective Tharp, John Lacey, Peter Nye) 102
   Assignment 26: Prosecutor and Plaintiffs' Attorney:
                  Skeleton Model
                  (Dr. Jackson, Dr. Day).. 103
   Assignment 27: Prosecutor and Plaintiffs' Attorney: Hospital
                  Records of Bruno Summers
                  (Rose Gadfly)... 104
   Assignment 28: Prosecutor and Plaintiffs' Attorney:
                  Weapons Applications and Check
                  (Fred Faye)... 105
   Assignment 29: Attorney for Defendant Hard: Scale
                  Diagram of the Gas Station
                  (John Gooding) 107
   Assignment 30: Attorney for Defendant Hard: Neo-Nazi
                  Membership Card
                  (Officer West, Rebecca Karr, Nurse Frank)........... 108

Assignment 31: Attorneys for Defendants Hard and Davola:
Death Certificate
(Dr. Day, Dr. Jackson) 109

Assignment 32: Attorney for Defendant Hard: Bruno
Summers's Knife
(Officer West, Nurse Frank) 111

Assignment 33: Prosecutor and Plaintiffs' Attorney:
Cross-Examination with a Prior Written
Statement and Prior Conviction
(Ed Hard) 112

Assignment 34: Attorney for Defendant Hard: Bruno
Summers's Blood Sample
(Officer Harris) 113

Assignment 35: Attorney for Defendant Hard: Courtroom
Demonstration
(Ed Hard) 115

Criminal Case Assignments
Assignment 36: Prosecutor: Gun, Rounds, and Slugs
(Officer Yale, Officer Harris, H. Tredwell) 116

Civil Case Assignments
Assignment 37: Plaintiffs' Attorney: Photographs
(Deborah Summers) 118

Assignment 38: Plaintiffs' Attorney: Hospital, Ambulance,
and Funeral Bills
(Deborah and Hans Summers, Rose Gadfly) 120

Assignment 39: Attorney for Defendant Hard: Medical
Records of Deborah Summers
(Dr. Sherman Croup) 121

Chapter 9. Direct Examination: Building the Case
Criminal Case Assignments
Assignment 40: Defense Attorney: Preparation of Direct
Examination
(John Gooding) 122

Assignment 41: Prosecutor: Direct Examination of
Fred Faye 123

Assignment 42: Prosecutor: Direct Examination of
Cindy Rigg 124

Assignment 43: Prosecutor: Direct Examination of
Roberta Montbank 125

Assignment 44: Prosecutor: Direct Examination of
Officer Yale
*(Breathalyzer Test; Alcohol Influence
Report; Opinion)* 126

Assignment 45: Defense Attorney: Direct Examination of
John Gooding
(August 26 and September 3 Incidents) 127

Civil Case Assignments

Assignment 46: Plaintiffs' Attorney: Preparation of Direct
Examination
(Deborah Summers) 128

Assignment 47: Attorney for Defendant Davola: Preparation
of Direct Examination
(Tom Donaldson) 130

Assignment 48: Plaintiffs' Attorney: Direct Examination of
Deborah Summers 131

Assignment 49: Plaintiffs' Attorney: Direct Examination of
Bert Kain 132

Assignment 50: Plaintiffs' Attorney: Direct Examination of
Roberta Montbank 133

Assignment 51: Plaintiffs' Attorney: Direct Examination of
Ronnie Summers
(Child Witness) 134

Assignment 52: Attorney for Defendant Hard: Direct
Examination of Ed Hard 135

Assignment 53: Attorney for Defendant Davola:
Direct Examination of Mary Apple 136

Chapter 10. Cross-Examination: Concession Seeking

Criminal Case Assignments

Assignment 54: Defense Attorney: Cross-Examination of
Peter Dean 137

Assignment 55: Defense Attorney: Cross-Examination of
Fred Faye 139

Assignment 56: Defense Attorney: Cross-Examination of
Cindy Rigg 140

Assignment 57: Defense Attorney: Cross-Examination of
Officer Yale 141

Assignment 58: Prosecutor: Cross-Examination of
John Gooding 142

Assignment 59: Prosecutor: Cross-Examination of Ed Hard 143

Civil Case Assignments

Assignment 60: Attorneys for Defendants Hard and Davola:
Cross-Examination of Deborah Summers 144

Assignment 61: Attorneys for Defendants Davola and Hard:
Cross-Examination of Bert Kain 145

Assignment 62: Attorneys for Defendants Davola and Hard:
Cross-Examination of Roberta Montbank 147

Assignment 63: Attorney for Defendant Hard:
                Cross-Examination of Ronnie Summers 148
Assignment 64: Plaintiffs' Attorney: Cross-Examination of
                Mary Apple 149
Assignment 65: Plaintiffs' Attorney: Cross-Examination of
                Ed Hard... 150

Chapter 11. Experts: Yours and Theirs
  Criminal Case Assignments
    Assignment 66: Prosecutor: Preparation of an Expert Witness
                    (Dr. L.R. Jackson, Medical Examiner)................. 152
    Assignment 67: Prosecutor and Defense Attorney:
                    Direct Examination and Cross-Examination
                    of an Expert Witness
                    (H. Tredwell, Firearms Expert) 153
    Assignment 68: Prosecutor and Defense Attorney:
                    Direct Examination and Cross-Examination
                    of an Expert Witness
                    (Dr. L.R. Jackson, Medical Examiner)................. 156
  Civil Case Assignments
    Assignment 69: Plaintiffs' Attorney: Preparation of an
                    Expert Witness
                    (Dr. Brett Day, Treating Physician)..................... 157
    Assignment 70: Plaintiffs' and Defendants' Attorneys:
                    Direct Examination and Cross-Examination
                    of an Expert Witness
                    (Dr. Brett Day, Treating Physician)..................... 159
    Assignment 71: Plaintiffs' and Defendants' Attorneys:
                    Direct Examination and Cross-Examination
                    of an Expert Witness
                    (Dr. Bruce Hann, Economist) 160
    Assignment 72: Defendants' and Plaintiffs' Attorneys:
                    Direct Examination and Cross-Examination
                    of an Expert Witness
                    (Dr. Thomas Monday, Economist) 162
    Assignment 73: Attorneys for Defendant Davola and
                    Plaintiffs: Direct Examination and
                    Cross-Examination of an Expert Witness
                    (Dr. Dale Thompson, Hospitality Expert)............. 164
    Assignment 74: Attorneys for Defendant Hard and Plaintiffs:
                    Direct Examination and Cross-Examination
                    of an Expert Witness
                    (Dr. Sherman Croup, Medical Doctor)................. 165

Chapter 12. Jury Instructions: The Jury's Law
  Criminal Case Assignments
    Assignment 75: Prosecutor: Preparation of Jury Instructions 167
    Assignment 76: Defense Attorney: Preparation of
                Jury Instructions 168
    Assignment 77: Prosecutor and Defense Attorney:
                Arguing Jury Instructions 169
  Civil Case Assignments
    Assignment 78: Plaintiffs' Attorney: Preparation of
                Jury Instructions and Verdict Forms;
                Arguing Instructions 171
    Assignment 79: Attorneys for Defendants Hard and Davola:
                Preparation of Jury Instructions and
                Verdict Forms; Arguing Instructions 173

Chapter 13. Closing Argument: Art of Argument
  Criminal Case Assignments
    Assignment 80: Prosecutor: Closing Argument 174
    Assignment 81: Defense Attorney: Closing Argument 176
  Civil Case Assignments
    Assignment 82: Plaintiffs' Attorney: Closing Argument 177
    Assignment 83: Attorney for Defendants Hard and
                Davola: Closing Argument 179

  The Final Assignment
    Assignment 84: Going to Trial—The Criminal or Civil Case:
                State v. Hard or *Summers v. Hard* 181

Appendix A: Checklists for Trial Skills
Chapter 2: Trial Persuasion Principles 183
Chapter 3: Case Theory and Theme Development 184
Chapter 4: Trial Motion Advocacy 188
Chapter 5: Making and Meeting Objections 192
Chapter 6: Jury Selection: Two-Way Exchange 194
Chapter 7: Opening Statement: Storytelling 196
Chapter 8: Exhibits and the Visual Trial 197
Chapter 9: Direct Examination: Building the Case 199
Chapter 10: Cross-Examination: Concession Seeking 202
Chapter 11: Experts: Yours and Theirs 205
Chapter 12: Jury Instructions: The Jury's Law 208
Chapter 13: Closing Arguments: Art of Argument 209

Appendix B: Trial Case File Table of Contents 211

Acknowledgments

The cover of this book indicates that it is the work of three authors. Yet there were truly so many other individuals—in so many capacities—who were essential to this book. Their combined contributions are visible to us on every page. We do more than thank them; we share credit with them for this work.

Nancy Ammons, coordinator of secretarial support and legal assistant, Seattle University School of Law.

Charlotte Anderson, copy center coordinator and business office accounts auditor.

Authors of *The Appellate Prosecutor.*

Mimy Bailey, Seattle University, class of 2007.

William S. Bill Bailey, attorney and adjunct professor, Seattle University School of Law.

Daniel Baker, law clerk, Seattle University School of Law, class of 2010.

Dorian S. Berger, Columbia University School of Law, class of 2008.

Mike Bitando, general manager of the Garage billiards hall and bowling.

Michael Caldwell, principal, Growth Industrie; Web designer and graphic artist.

Brady Clark, professor of linguistics, Northwestern University.

Clancy Clark, M.D.

Colby Clark, graphics designer.

Nancy Clark, artist and editor.

Fred DeKay, adjunct professor of law, Seattle University School of Law.

Dean E. Edwin Eck, Director Karen Townsend, and the faculty of the University of Montana Law School's Advanced Trial Advocacy Program.

Anne Enquist, associate director of legal writing, Seattle University School of Law.

Justin Farmer, law clerk, Seattle University School of Law, class of 2009.

Kerry Fitz-Gerald, associate librarian, Seattle University School of Law.

Tyler Fox, instructional technology manager, Center for Educational Leadership, University of Washington.

Steve Fury, attorney at law.

Captain Tag Gleason, Seattle Police Department, Violent Crimes Section.

Monica Hartsock, law clerk, Seattle University School of Law, class of 2009.

Daniel Jackson, Seattle University, class of 2008; and Carol Jackson, with Katie, Briana, Ryan, and Sean Jackson.

Sarah Johnson, attorney at law.

The Honorable Judge Ronald Kessler, King County Superior Court.

The Honorable Judge Robert S. Lasnik, Chief Judge, the United States District Court, Western District of Washington.

Law students at Seattle University School of Law.

Gretchen Ludwig, director of the Garage movie and the Freck Point trial movie, both on DVD.

The Honorable Judge Terrance Lukens, JAMS (Judicial Arbitration Mediation Services); adjunct professor of Law, Seattle University School of Law.

The Honorable Judge Dean Lum, King County Superior Court; adjunct professor of law, at Seattle University School of Law.

Deborah Maenhout, actor, the Freck Point trial movie.

Dr. Norman Mar, Ph.D.

Lisa Marchese, attorney and adjunct professor, Seattle University School of Law.

Terry McAdam, laboratory manager, Washington State crime laboratory and actor.

Hannalore Merritt, Seattle University School of Law, class of 2009.

Rebecca Miller, officer, Seattle Police Department, East Precinct.

Melissa (Missy) Mordy, actor, Seattle University School of Law, class of 2009.

The Honorable Judge Dean Morgan; Distinguished Jurist in Residence, Seattle University School of Law.

Theodore Myhre, lecturer, University of Washington School of Law.

National College of District Attorneys faculty.

The Honorable Judge Jack Nevin, Pierce County District Court; adjunct professor of Law, Seattle University School of Law.

Laurel Oates, professor of law and director of legal writing, Seattle University School of Law.

Kyle C. Olive, attorney at law.

Rex Prout, assistant chief of enforcement and education, Washington State Liquor Control Board.

Ryan Rautio, law clerk, Seattle University School of Law, class of 2010.

Kristin Richardson, senior deputy, King County Prosecutor's Office; adjunct professor of law, Seattle University School of Law.

Michael V. Riggio, attorney; adjunct professor of law, Seattle University School of Law.

Ann Rule, true crime author.

Nora Santos, administrative assistant, Seattle University School of Law.

Vonda M. Sargent, attorney; adjunct professor of law, Seattle University School of Law.

Kirk Van Scoyoc, actor.

Richard Sherwin, professor of law and director, New York Law School's Visual Persuasion Project.

Craig Sims, attorney; adjunct professor of law, Seattle University School of Law.

Laurie Sleeper, administrative assistant, Seattle University School of Law.

John Jay Syverson, photographer, OnPoint Productions, Seattle.

Travis Ronald Tillman, law clerk, Seattle University School of Law, class of 2010.

Melinda Tilton, Department of Communications and Theater, Montana State University, Billings.

The Honorable Judge Michael Trickey, King County Superior Court.

Justin Walsh, law clerk, Seattle University School of Law, class of 2008.

Matt Williams, attorney; adjunct professor of law, Seattle University School of Law.

Ric Wyant, forensic scientist, Firearm/Toolmark Section, Crime Laboratory Division; firearms examiner for the Washington State Patrol Crime Laboratory.

A special thank you for the assistance we were provided at Seattle University School of Law: Dean Kellye Testy, Vice Dean Annette Clark, Associate Dean for Finance and Administration Richard Bird, Kristin Cheney, Associate Dean for Library and Educational Technology, Stephanie Zimmerman, Director of Instructional Technology, and J. Barratt Godfrey, multimedia specialist.

And finally, thanks to our friends and professional colleagues at Aspen Publishers: Carol McGeehan, publisher; Steve Errick, managing director; John Devins, developmental editor; Carmen Corral-Reid, senior editor; Michael A. Gregory, director of sales and marketing for legal education; and Lisa Wehrle, manuscript editor.

Trial Advocacy

Assignments and Case Files

1 *Introduction to the Books, CDs, DVD, and Web Site*

I. INTRODUCTION

A. Overview

Trial Advocacy: Assignments and Case Files provides detailed and realistic role-play performance assignments that replicate trial practice. Its companion text, *Trial Advocacy: Planning Analysis and Strategy* (the text) provides a rich approach to thinking about, planning, and performing as a practicing trial lawyer. The wide range of trial practice situations presented in the text foster the kinds of analytic processes and skills needed to perform trial work, while transporting you into the trial lawyer's world.

This introduction to the books, CDs, DVD, and Web site provides a basic understanding of how each component is structured and intended to be used.

B. The Books

Trial Advocacy: Assignments and Case Files

Trial Advocacy: Assignments and Case Files contain 84 criminal and civil assignments. The *Assignment* book and the case files are intended for professional workshops and legal education trial advocacy classes. Together they provide an opportunity for performance role-plays that simulate a range of adversarial practice situations, such as making an opening statement, introducing an exhibit, cross-examining a witness, and so on. A CD with Case Files for two fictitious cases—*State v. Hard* and *Summers v. Hard*—is contained in the jacket pocket in the back of this book. The performances in the assignments are based on these two cases that share a single but complex fact pattern that manifests itself in both a criminal homicide and a civil wrongful death case.

Each assignment refers to portions of the text, *Trial Advocacy: Planning Analysis and Strategy* (referred to as *Trial Advocacy* text); to documents from the case files that are on the CD; and to sections of the State of Major Rules of Evidence that are identical to the Federal Rules of Evidence, Civil Procedure, and Criminal Procedure. Included in the assignments are "Tips for this Assignment," intended as practice pointers. These *Tips* refer to strategic considerations for performing the skill and point to substantive and ethical issues that might arise in similar situations in actual practice.

Accompanying the assignments are checklists that provide a quick reminder of the suggested approach to the various skills. The checklists refer to chapters in the *Trial Advocacy* text.

Trial Advocacy: Planning, Analysis and Strategy

Trial Advocacy: Planning Analysis and Strategy (the ***Trial Advocacy*** **text)** is a trial advocacy text consisting of 13 chapters. Each chapter covers a separate trial subject area—for example, trial persuasion, jury selection, opening statement, objections, exhibits, direct examination, and so on. The text presents both a theoretical approach and a practice-oriented approach for trial skills. The book includes extensive illustrations, hypothetical situations, and imparts practical and strategic pointers in the subject areas. The text also includes references to sources in the practice area that detail developments in the use of technology in the modern trial lawyer's practice.

C. Icons and Boxes

Throughout the chapters, boxes appear containing information and covering topics and facts of a hypothetical, illustration of a point, ethical rules, statutes, or procedural rules. The topical material within each box is designated by the following symbols:

Checklists

Facts of a Hypothetical

Illustration of a Point

Pointers

Ethical Rules, Statutes, or Procedural Rules

II. THE CDs

A. Case Files

The Case Files CD is found in the back cover of the *Assignments* book and contains the criminal and civil case files for *State v. Hard* and *Summers v. Hard*. Included are pleadings, diagrams, documents, expert reports, jury instructions, research memoranda, statutes, and witness statements, and a PowerPoint presentation.

The research memoranda are a special feature. The memoranda are composed of fictional cases from the fictional jurisdiction, the State of Major. The memos provide the research you need to deal with the multitude of legal issues in the assignments. Of course, your instructor may prefer that you instead research and use appropriate cases and statutes from your jurisdiction. A table of contents of the CD is on the CD and also in Appendix B on pages 211-216 of this book. The CD allows you to print individual documents or the entire case file.

B. The Actors' Guide

To make the assignments' role-playing simulations as realistic as possible, the Actors' Guide CD given to your instructor contains information for distribution to the role-players. For instance, in one role-play, someone in the class will play a lay witness being examined on direct; in another, the student will play an expert who is cross-examined. Background materials detailing the lay witness's personal history, the instructions for how the witness is to behave and respond, the expert's background, and a summary of the particular area of expertise are part of these materials.

III. THE DVD: MOVIE OF A TRIAL AND THE SCENE OF THE CRIME

A DVD accompanies the *Trial Advocacy: Planning Analysis and Strategy* book. The DVD presents experienced trial lawyers demonstrating a trial, specifically, the *Freck* Wrongful Death case. The Freck murder case, which precedes the civil case, is loosely based on the real case, which is the subject of the noted true crime writer Ann Rule's book, *A Rose for Her Grave* (True Crime Files) (Time Warner Paperbacks, 1995). These demonstrations are intended to aid you when you perform the same skills in the assignments. There is also the *Scene of the Crime* movie that takes you to the Garage tavern where the fictitious *State v. Hard* and *Summers v. Hard* cases all began.

IV. WEB SITE

There is a Web site for the Pretrial and Trial books that displays supplementary material and useful visuals. See *www.aspenadvocacybooks.com*.

V. RULES OF THE GAME

In performing the role-play assignments, we have created a mythical state, city, and counties, along with fictitious people who reside, work, live, and die in these mythical places. These places may resemble a place that you may live in or have visited, or have read about or seen on TV. Yet, even though it is a mythical locale, we hope you remember it fondly as you proceed through life with the skills you have learned. So with that in mind, here are the Rules of the Game.

A. Jurisdiction

These two fictitious cases, *State v. Hard* and *Summers v. Hard*, take place in the jurisdiction of the State of Major. The specific setting encompasses the adjoining counties of Jamner and Neva. The City of Ruston is within the

County of Jamner. Neva City is the main city in Neva County. The jurisdiction of the State of Major was chosen for a number of reasons. Its laws reflect, although they are probably not identical with, current law on the various issues raised in the cases. The memorandum opinions in the jurisdiction of Major are brief and to the point, replacing what would be hundreds of pages in other jurisdictions with a small fraction of that volume. The opinions, nevertheless, require careful reading and interpretation. They provide a foundation for the assignments, whose purpose is to teach you how to think about a body of law in an active adversary context, rather than to teach you substantive criminal and civil procedure and doctrine. Do not do any outside research unless your instructor tells you otherwise.

B.   Evidentiary, Procedural, and Professional Responsibility Rules

The State of Major Court Rules and Rules of Criminal and Civil Procedure are in most instances identical to the Federal Rules of Civil Procedure and the Federal Rules of Criminal Procedure. The Major Evidence Code is identical to the Federal Rules of Evidence. The standards of professional responsibility in the State of Major are based on the ABA Model Rules of Professional Conduct. These latter rules are intended to provide a legal structure in which you can analyze the particular ethical situations in the assignments. Of course, your instructor may instead ask you to deal with the ethical situations under the current rules in your jurisdiction.

C.   Dates

The fictitious incidents take place in the following years:

20XX   Last year—the year that the shooting took place.
20XX +   Years after last year (20XX + 1 is this year).
20XX −   Years prior to the incident (20XX − 2 is three years ago).

To give the cases a feeling of reality, the dates in the case files should be converted into actual dates, so that "20XX + 4" is changed to four years after last year's date. If last year was 2008, that would mean 20XX + 4 = 2012.

D.   Civil Case

Whenever you deal with the civil case, *Summers v. Hard*, you should assume that the criminal case has been disposed of in such a manner that the main character, Ed Hard, cannot legitimately resist answering in the civil case by claiming that he will incriminate himself.

E. Your Responsibilities

As a class member or as an attorney assigned to conduct a particular performance, your own good sense and the directions of your instructor will make your responsibilities clear. Your responsibilities when role-playing a witness, however, are a different matter. The quality of your effort in preparation, and in the subsequent performance of your role, can make or break the class. Effort put into your role-playing can make witness examination come alive by challenging the planning and performance skills of the student who is playing the attorney. Lack of effort and enthusiasm can result in an unrealistic, fragmented, boring shambles.

As a witness, you have two responsibilities:

1. *Preparation:* You should prepare for your witness performance by reviewing the assignment and readings, and the pretrial case file documents listed for the assignment for which you are playing the role of a witness. Your instructor also may assign confidential witness information from the Actors' Guide (a detailed witness profile, witness instructions, and special documents). Be certain to bring to class all your witness information.

2. *Innovation:* Although we have tried to make the materials as complete as possible, there may be circumstances in which the factual materials furnished to you are insufficient. Therefore, you will have to be somewhat innovative at times. If you are asked questions on matters not covered by the facts you have been furnished, you may add any facts that are consistent with the supplied facts. You may also add details that provide color and reality to your character. You should *not* add a fact, however, that would be so important that it might affect the outcome of the lawsuit. If in doubt, ask your instructor.

Depending on the actual selection, sequence, and performance of the assignments in your class, you may encounter gaps in information or may fail to make the acquaintance of some of the witnesses who figure in the principal cases. It has been our experience that such potential gaps in information do not constitute real difficulties; however, be certain to consult your instructor if you are uncertain.

F.   The Game

We have just discussed the rules of the game for the performance assignments. Because it is a game, no clients will go to prison for life. No one will lose a home or business or be denied access to his children. So feel free to play because, ironically, the more you play, the better you will do when you enter the real world of trial work. Work hard at your play. Your clients are awaiting you in the next few years, and they are completely and totally dependent on you and on your having learned your lessons well.

We hope you like using this book and the accompanying materials and that you enjoy living with the characters as much as we enjoyed creating them. If any character or situation reminds you of someone you know, so much the better for the game to seem real. It is not our intention, however, to represent any real person or situation; this is a work of fiction.

VI.   FACTUAL SUMMARY: *STATE v. HARD* AND *SUMMERS v. HARD*

The following factual summary gives you an overview of what happened in *Summers v. Hard* and *State v. Hard*. These cases are the basis for the Assignments 1 through 84. This is a composite highlighting what some of the witnesses claim occurred. For specifics and greater detail, refer to the documents in the case files, which are contained in the CD that is in the jacket pocket of this book.

During the evening of August 20 of last year, Bruno Summers and his fiancée, Deborah Miller, were in the Garage, a tavern in the City of Ruston, State of Major. The Garage has both a bowling alley and pool hall on different sides of the building. Bruno and Deborah were seated in the bar area adjacent to the pool hall. The Garage tavern is owned by M. C. Davola and his wife. Edward Taylor Hard also was in the tavern that day. Ed Hard, allegedly intoxicated and boisterous, approached the Summers-Miller table and began making advances toward Deborah Miller, his former girlfriend. Bruno Summers and Deborah Miller rose to pay the bill and leave. Ed Hard grabbed Bruno Summers around the neck, and a struggle ensued. Bruno Summers knocked Hard to the floor, splitting Hard's lip and chipping a tooth. Bartender Tom Donaldson ordered both men to leave the tavern. Tavern patrons overheard the exchange between Summers and Hard and saw what happened.

At the time of the August 20 incident, Bruno Summers was 30 years old and the owner of University Fitness Center. He also was a member of a neo-Nazi organization. Ed Hard was 27 years of age, and he worked as a house painter.

On August 22, Ed Hard went to the American Gun Shop located in Neva, Major, and he purchased a .22-caliber revolver. On August 27, after the statutory five-day waiting period had passed, Hard paid for and received the gun and bought some ammunition. On the same day—the 27th—Bruno Summers married Deborah Miller. This was Bruno Summers's second marriage. His first marriage lasted six years, and he was awarded custody of his two children by that marriage, Ronnie, age 8, and Amanda, age 12.

On September 3 of last year, at approximately 8:00 P.M., Ed Hard and two friends, John Gooding and Rebecca Karr, were in the Garage tavern seated at the bar. They had several drinks before arriving at the tavern. Bartender Donaldson served them rounds of drinks. They were talking loudly. Bruno Summers, his new wife Deborah Summers, and their friend Peter Dean entered the pool hall side of the Garage tavern at approximately 9:00 P.M. They had spent the previous couple of hours on the bowling side of the Garage tavern, where they bowled and drank. The three walked to the entrance of the bar area and saw Hard sitting at the bar. Hard was overheard making a comment about the presence of the Summers in the tavern. Deborah wanted to leave, but Bruno said that instead they would sit in a booth near the front of the tavern, some distance away from Hard.

Roughly five minutes after the Summers and Peter Dean entered the pool hall side of the Garage, Bruno got up from the booth and went to the restroom near the front door of the tavern. Hard confronted Bruno Summers as he left the restroom. An exchange took place. Hard produced a gun and shot Bruno Summers. Deborah ran to her husband, who lay bleeding on the tavern floor. The bartender called 911. Hard immediately left the Garage.

Peter Dean called Hans Summers, Bruno Summers's father, who along with his wife Gretchen were at Bruno and Deborah's house taking care of their two grandchildren, Ronnie and Amanda. The grandparents loaded the two children into the car and drove to the Garage, where they parked on the street in front of the pool hall side of the tavern. Hans Summer went to the front door of the tavern, where he was stopped by a Ruston police officer who told him that he would have to wait while the EMTs took care of his son. Hans Summers could see his son's bleeding body from the doorway. His daughter-in-law was standing near Bruno's body, and she was crying and screaming. Hans Summers looked down to find that his grandson had left the car and was standing at his side. When Ronnie saw his father, he also began screaming and crying. Bruno's parents and children followed the ambulance to Mercy Hospital where Bruno was admitted for treatment.

Ruston police officers were dispatched to Hard's residence, where they entered without a warrant, arrested Hard, and seized a revolver that later a firearm's expert was able to match with the slug recovered from Bruno's body. The officers took Hard to the precinct, where detective Russell Tharp took a statement from him. In that statement, Hard, among other things, said that he had feared for his life and shot Summers by accident. Also, a breathalyzer test was administered, and Hard's blood alcohol level was .16.

Both Deborah and eight-year-old Ronnie Summers suffered emotional disturbances from witnessing what happened to Bruno Summers. They both saw a psychologist, who, after administering a battery of tests, opined that they suffer from post-traumatic stress disorder.

Bruno Summers at first seemed to be recovering from the gunshot wound. However, he contracted pneumonia and died on September 7. Ed Hard was charged by information with murder in the first degree. Plaintiffs Hans and Gretchen Summers, individually and as personal representatives of Bruno's estate and guardians of the children, and Deborah filed a complaint for damages against defendants Edward Hard, M.C. Davola and his wife, waitress Mary Apple, bartender, and the Garage tavern.

At first the case was handled by another lawyer in your firm. That lawyer has since taken a leave of absence from the office to trek through Argentina. As you first enter the cases, discovery has been completed in both the civil and criminal case, and efforts to bargain a favorable disposition in the criminal case and to negotiate a settlement in the civil case have failed. These cases are going to trial.

2 *Trial Preparation and Case Management*

"[Preparation] is the be-all of good trial work. Everything else—felicity of expression, improvisational brilliance—is a satellite around the sun. Thorough preparation is that sun."

Louis Nizer, quoted in *The New Lawyer's Wit and Wisdom: Quotations on the Legal Profession, in Brief* 269 (Bruce Nash & Allan Zullo eds., Kathryn Zullo comp., Running Press 2001)

"It's in the preparation—in those dreary pedestrian virtues they taught you in seventh grade and you didn't believe. It's making the extra call and caring a lot."

Diane Sawyer, quoted in *The Book of Positive Quotations* 589 (Steve Deger & Leslie Ann Gibson eds., John Cook comp., 2d ed., Fairview Press 2007)

I.   INTRODUCTION

When called on, you rise, look the judge in the eye, and announce, "Ready for trial, Your Honor." Trial preparation—and indeed this book and its companion (the text)—are dedicated to ensuring that when you say you are ready, you truly are; that you have thoroughly prepared and are confident that you will prevail. Thorough preparation is the foundation for success in trial.

Getting to this state of readiness is challenging. Trial preparation is laborious. It means that the advocate has pursued a complete factual investigation, is organized, and has a command of the law and facts. Trial preparation encompasses a variety of activities, including fact investigation, legal research, and application of strategies for organizing and rapidly retrieving the information. Trial preparations also involve preparing and rehearsing each phase of trial from motions' advocacy through closing argument.

Here, you will learn about areas important to trial preparation: case development, legal research, the selection and utilization of experts during the investigation, the search for and preservation of physical evidence, and ethical considerations during the investigation. We also cover how to manage your case information in an orderly manner so that you understand what information you have and know how to retrieve it easily. You will be introduced to an organizational tool we call a fact-development diagram, see page 17. This diagram provides an approach to investigation as well as a system for organizing both the investigation and the information you uncover. Finally, we offer techniques and trial systems for organizing and managing the case, with an emphasis on electronic case management software.

You may recognize some of the case development information in this chapter if you are familiar with our *Pretrial Advocacy* book. The material is reiterated here because it is every bit as important to trial as it is to pretrial advocacy. If you have read some of this information before, we hope this serves as a refresher before you delve into the new material pertinent to preparing for trial.

II.   PLANNING CASE DEVELOPMENT

A.   Case Theory as a Guide

Case development is a critical part of trial preparation. All case development activities are aimed at a single objective: finding information that bears on the legal and factual components of the case theory and developing a comparable appreciation of the opposing side's case theory. In this investigation, you are hunting for information both favorable and unfavorable because you want to understand the case's weaknesses as well as its strengths.

Particularly at the outset of case development, you must be open to finding factual evidence that will modify, or even change, your factual theory to such an extent that the legal theory must change. Indeed, early in the case, your search for the facts will aid you in selecting among competing legal theories or in deciding to abandon a legal theory.

To illustrate the importance of an investigation of the facts and the gathering of evidence to support your legal theory, assume that you are considering representing the plaintiff, 23-year-old Litonya Barefoot, in the *Bicyclist-Crosswalk* case.

CASE THEORY AS A GUIDE TO INVESTIGATION

The *Bicyclist-Crosswalk* Case

Litonya Barefoot has told you that she was commuting by bicycle to Major University on October 11, where she is a graduate student in psychology. As is her typical habit, she crossed the arterial of 12th Avenue in a westbound direction, which immediately adjoins the campus. There are two westbound crosswalks at the intersection of 12th and Marion, where the collision occurred. There is a flashing yellow light up above to catch the attention of motorists. There is neither a stop sign for northbound nor for southbound traffic on 12th Avenue. Barefoot was hit while in the crosswalk, sustaining injury to her right shoulder and left hip.

After meeting with Barefoot, you request a copy of the police report of this incident.

Your initial legal theory is that the motorist, James Tyler Sullivan, was negligent in that he failed to see the bicyclist in the marked crosswalk and did not yield the right-of-way to her. As a necessary prerequisite to developing your legal theory, you must first research the applicable law for the right-of-way in crosswalks. You find the following statute in the motor vehicle code:

CROSSWALKS

STATUTE

(1) The operator of an approaching vehicle shall stop and remained stopped to allow a pedestrian or bicycle to cross the roadway within an unmarked or marked crosswalk when the pedestrian or bicycle is upon or within one lane of a half of the roadway upon which the vehicle is traveling or onto which it is turning.

(2) No pedestrian or bicycle shall suddenly leave a curb or other place of safety and walk, run, or otherwise move into the path of a vehicle which is so close that it is impossible for the driver to stop.

After reviewing the pertinent statute governing the right-of-way to support your legal theory, you then want to construct your factual theory. You begin by reviewing the police report. You learn that Sullivan received a citation and the matter is currently pending. You also find out that because of an increased focus on pedestrian and bicycle safety in the jurisdiction, this case was worked up thoroughly by the police. It includes the investigating officer's report, which includes a narrative, witness statements, a cell phone photograph taken by a bystander immediately after the collision (shown below), visibility photographs, and a live action study on videotape.

The investigating officer, Kim Jarvis, reached the conclusion that James Tyler Sullivan should have been able to see the bicyclist, yielding the right-of-way and avoiding the collision. You decide to take the case of Ms. Barefoot.

You want to argue the following factual theory: that the bicyclist was in the crosswalk and that the oncoming car failed to yield the right-of-way; your client left the curb and entered the crosswalk at a time when it was safe to do so, when it was possible for an oncoming driver to stop. You can make this factual argument only because the evidence according to your preliminary reading of the police report supports this as a tentative factual theory. However, you still need to investigate further to gather all the facts. If additional evidence exists contradicting these factual assertions of liability by the motorist, your legal and factual theory might be weak or even be without factual support to the extent that the case may lack merit.

B.   Researching Legal Theories

For plaintiff's counsel, the question might be: "Which comes first—the facts or the law?" The answer is: "The facts." The client provides the factual story and seeks counsel's legal advice. Counsel begins with at least some initial research to determine what legal theories may be viable. On the other hand, defense counsel's starting point is the law as asserted by the plaintiff; research into the law and then investigation of the facts flows from there. As the case is developed factually, more expansive and in-depth research is conducted.

It is beyond the scope of any single book to explore all the potential substantive laws that might be the basis for lawsuits, defenses, or all procedures. It is up to you, as the advocate, to determine the law applicable to your client's situation.

PRETRIAL RESEARCH AREAS

Your trial preparation research will cover a broad range of subjects, such as these:

- **Forum:** Where (federal or state court and venue within the jurisdiction);
- **Timing:** When to file (the statute of limitations);
- **Procedure:** How to plead and serve process (joinder of parties, claims, capacity to sue, service of process);
- **Substantive law** governing the legal theory component of your case theory: What action or defense (negligence, comparative negligence, products liability, contracts, murder, conspiracy, and so forth); and
- **Evidentiary matters:** Admissibility of evidence (suppression of unlawfully seized evidence under the Fourth Amendment, authenticity of a document) under rules of evidence.

Research Resources

You may well begin and end your research online using Westlaw or LEXIS. This computerized research will get you into applicable case law, statutes, and court rules. The following are illustrative pretrial Internet links that also are useful.

USEFUL INTERNET LINKS

- ABA Civil Discovery Standards—*http://www.abanet.org/litigation/discoverystandards/home.html*
- ABA Model Rules of Professional Conduct—*http://www.abanet.org/cpr/mrpc/mrpc_toc.html*

---

continues ▶

- Federal Rules of Civil Procedure—*http://www.law.cornell.edu/rules/frcp/index.html*
- Federal Rules of Criminal Procedure—*http://straylight.law.cornell.edu/rules/frcrmp/*
- Federal Rules of Evidence—*http://www.law.cornell.edu/rules/fre/index.html*

Your research may delve into hornbooks (a nice start to research because they provide overviews of the subject matter), law reviews, American Law Reports (A.L.R.), statutes, court rules, and other practice materials.

C.   Organizing the Fact Investigation

We suggest a fact-development diagram that will help you organize and conduct your factual investigation. If you represent the plaintiff, the chart begins with column 1 listing the elements of your legal theory (negligence). Column 2 lists the principal factual assertions to support the elements of the legal theory. Column 3 lists the evidence that supports or detracts from your assertions. Columns 4 and 5 are the sources of the evidence (witnesses, documents) and the investigative method (witness interviews) that could be used to uncover the evidence. Column 6 contains the evidentiary concerns you have about the admissibility of that evidence. See page 17.

For defense counsel, the first column contains the elements of the plaintiff's legal theory that the defense can attack and/or the elements of affirmative defenses (comparative fault, also referred to as contributory negligence). If the first column contains the elements of the plaintiff's claim, the second column would contain factual assertions that could be used to attack the elements. Otherwise, the subject matter for each column remains the same as the plaintiff's diagram.

When you fill in this fact-development diagram, you will have an organizational tool that structures the investigation and provides you with an overview of the case. This diagram will direct you to what (factual information you need to acquire), where (the source to go for the information), and the investigative method to use. To learn how to complete the diagram and use it to organize and plan case development, see the illustration on the *Bicyclist-Crosswalk* case (page 30).

By filling in the diagram, you see graphically what evidence you have and what evidence you are missing. When you have determined what you are missing, you can brainstorm to determine what the possible sources are for the evidence. And you can prepare a to-do investigation checklist.

FACT-DEVELOPMENT DIAGRAM—FOR PLAINTIFFS OR DEFENDANTS					
1. Elements	**2. Factual Allegations**	**3. Evidence**	**4. Sources of Information**	**5. Investigation Method**	**6. Evidentiary Concerns**
Plaintiff's legal theory (divide into elements) Or ***Defendant's legal theory*** (divide into elements of plaintiffs legal theory that are subject to attack; also list separately each element of any affirmative or other defenses)	**Plaintiff's or defendant's factual theory:** factual or opinion assertions supporting each element	**Evidence** that could support or attack the factual assertions underlying each element	**Sources** of information	**Case development method**	**Evidentiary concerns** with this information (and the specific information for any evidentiary foundations required to meet such concerns)

D. Avoiding Tunnel Vision

At the outset of case development, your legal research and fact investigation should be far-reaching and broad enough to consider all possibilities. You are engaged in the process of shaping factual theories that might support the potential legal theories you are sifting through. In this hunt for supporting facts, you must remain open-minded. If you find evidence that modifies or even changes your factual theory, be willing to alter your legal theory. Thus, you should be ready to question and revise your understanding of the incident based on newly uncovered evidence. It is essential that you not develop tunnel vision that will prevent you from perceiving or looking for new evidence or new legal theories.

While you never want to develop tunnel vision, you should consider narrowing your focus as the case develops. When you have settled on a legal theory, you can prepare a fact-development diagram and plan a thorough investigation. If you represent the plaintiff, you will devote your investigation to uncovering evidence that both support and detracts from the elements of your legal theory. If you represent the defendant, you will concentrate on how to attack the elements of the plaintiff's legal theory and/or search for evidence that supports or weakens your affirmative defense. The search is not just for facts that are legally sufficient to support the legal theory. The search is also for the second part of the factual theory—facts that will persuade the jury. As part of your initial investigation, you will want to collect and preserve evidence that may be used in preparation of your case, for settlement, or for trial.

Once you know the basic facts and applicable law in the *Bicyclist-Crosswalk* case, it is important to personally visit the scene and observe traffic conditions, motorist and pedestrian behavior patterns, and sight lines. For example, do pedestrians typically have to challenge motorists at this location to get their attention by moving into the crosswalk or by attempting to make eye contact? Do pedestrians typically look both ways? How busy is this intersection? How congested is traffic at the time of the event in issue? Do cars generally drive slower or faster than the posted speed? Drive your own car on the same route as the motorist did that day. How visible are pedestrians as you approach the intersection? Are there any obstructions that prevent the driver or bicyclist from being clearly seen? Stand on the corner in the position of the bicyclist. How far away can oncoming cars clearly be seen? How long does it take a pedestrian or bicyclist to cross this street? How long does it take a motorist to stop, once a pedestrian is seen? How adequate are the traffic controls and signs at this location?

It is important to turn your instincts loose and process everything that is happening in the scene around you, becoming an expert on it. Once you have had adequate time to process the scene, take photographs to illustrate the patterns, behaviors, and physical facts that your senses and instincts have given you, paying particular attention to how such photographs will both support and detract from your legal theory. Don't just look for what favors your client's position. Part of avoiding tunnel vision is anticipating what facts and theories will be available to your opponent. Better to know these from the very beginning, if possible, developing effective responses to them as you build your case.

E.   Focus Groups—Testing the Facts

Tunnel vision can result with even the most careful analysis and investigation. It is human nature to look for facts that are consistent with an opinion and reject or ignore those that are inconsistent. While the lawyer develops a working hypothesis that seems sound, lay people at trial or your adversary during settlement talks might not believe the story.

For this reason, some lawyers use a marketing research tool—the focus group. You assemble a group of people obtained through a newspaper advertisement and present basic facts about your case to them. For example, in the *Bicyclist-Crosswalk* case, you might show them photos of the intersection, the police report, and the witness statements, summarizing the factual contentions of both sides and the applicable law. Each member of the group would then answer a questionnaire about which side would prevail and why, the credibility of each side's theories and contentions, and whether additional information about the case is needed before making a decision about who would prevail. Once the individual questionnaires are completed, you then have the focus group discuss the case while you videotape the discussion. Well in advance of trial, the focus group will identify your hot-button issues and whether your legal theory is on the right track. It will also tell you what the demographics of your ideal decision makers might be. In fact, some lawyers do focus groups on big-budget, important cases before agreeing to represent the client, learning if there are significant unseen problems that would make representation unwise.

F.   Resource Factors

When you set out to develop the case, you will want to prepare an estimate of how much your legal research and the fact investigation will cost. Your client will want to know how much it will cost and how you arrived at the dollar figure. The answers depend on how far you go with the case. If you negotiate a settlement shortly after a complaint is filed, the cost will be low when compared with the expense of full pretrial and trial.

Even if you are a prosecutor, a publicly funded defense attorney, or an attorney working on a contingent fee basis who will not log billable hours for your case development work, you still have to keep in mind the resources you may require. In criminal prosecution and defense, you must balance the significance of the case (death penalty versus first-time shoplift) against available public resources in even conceptualizing the scope and manner of your legal and factual investigation. If you are a civil attorney taking a case on a contingent fee, you could go broke if you fail to realistically estimate how much a case will cost you in terms of your time and office resources.

You should estimate the number of hours you will spend on each of these activities:

- Legal research,
- Investigation of the facts,
- Pleadings,
- Discovery,
- Pretrial hearings,
- Settlement discussions,
- Trial preparation, and
- Trial.

In addition to determining the cost of your services by multiplying the number of billable hours times your hourly rate, you should calculate the case costs including, among other things:

- Court clerk filing fees,
- Investigator's fee,
- Expert witness fee, and
- Court reporter fees for depositions.

G. Informal and Formal Fact Investigation

Civil Case Development

Civil case development methods fall into these two categories: (1) informal case development and (2) initial disclosure and formal discovery. They subdivide further as follows:

CIVIL CASE DEVELOPMENT
METHODS CHECKLIST

Informal Fact Investigation

- Client interview
- Witness interviews
- Scene visit
- Expert witness consultation
- Scientific testing by expert
- Development of demonstrative evidence
- Demand for access to public records under law (such as the Freedom of Information Act)
- Request for disclosure to counsel

Discovery: Initial Disclosure and Formal Discovery

Required Initial Disclosure—Rule 26(a)
Interrogatories—Rule 33
Requests for Production—Rule 34
Medical/Mental Examinations—Rule 35
Subpoena Duces Tecum—Rule 45
Depositions—Rules 27-32
Requests for Admissions—Rule 36

Civil Motions: referenced to the relevant Federal Rules of Civil Procedure

- Lack of subject matter—Rule 12(b)(1)
- Lack of personal jurisdiction—Rule 12(b)(2)
- Improper venue—Rule 12(b)(3)
- Improper service of process—Rule 12(b)(5)
- Failure to state a claim—Rule 12(b)(6)
- Failure to join an indispensable party—Rule 12(b)(7)
- Judgment on the pleadings—Rule 12(c)
- Voluntary dismissal—Rule 41(a)
- Involuntary dismissal for failure to prosecute, comply with the Rules or a court order—Rule 41(b)

continues ▶

> - Default judgment—Rule 55(a)
> - Set aside default judgment—Rule 55(c)
> - Summary judgment—Rule 56

For any given case, you will probably use both formal and informal fact investigation. Informal fact investigation has a number of advantages, as follows.

- First, it's *inexpensive* (a phone call, walking over to someone's office). In contrast, a formal discovery device like a deposition is expensive. Even devices like interrogatories can run up the bill for the client when the attorney is being paid by the hour for their preparation and evaluation.

- Second, it's *simple*. No formal devices or procedural hoops are involved as is the case with activities such as drafting and serving a subpoena duces tecum or request for production of documents. Again, informal fact-gathering can be a walk through the site of a collision or a meeting over a cup of coffee at a café.

- Third, it's *unbounded in time, scope, or location* by any formal legal rules. Formal discovery generally may not take place prior to the filing of the complaint. Interrogatories, depositions, and such may be served or scheduled only within timelines explicitly set by the Federal Rules of Civil Procedure and its state counterparts. Informal investigation can be done at any time you choose, before or after a formal action is filed. Also, formal discovery rules have limits as to target or location. Some devices are limited to parties (such as requests for admissions are limited parties); others are limited as to the geographic radius under which some device can be used (such as a subpoena to appear at deposition). Informal discovery has no such constraints as to either target or location.

- Fourth, informal fact investigation can be *done without announcing* that you are seeking information as part of a lawsuit. A witness may be far more candid if he doesn't understand that his statements may be eventually used for the filing or support of a legal claim. Of course, you must be aware of the ethical rules circumscribing dealing with represented witnesses, potential parties, and nonparties.

- Fifth, it can be *quicker and easier* than with a formal discovery method such as deposition. Thus, you could go through all the trouble of drafting a subpoena duces tecum for the witness to bring a document to the deposition. Or you could just call opposing counsel and ask for the document.

- Sixth, the *case may not require much in the way of formal discovery* because the evidence is readily available without having to seek it from the opposing party. For instance, informal fact investigation is especially suitable for gathering evidence from neutral or cooperative witnesses.

For example, in the *Bicyclist-Crosswalk* case, your informal fact investigation activities could include the following:

- An interview with your client Litonya Barefoot to determine what happened;
- Interviews of eyewitnesses listed on the police report;
- Visits to the scene of the collision, where you observe traffic patterns, times, and distances;
- A drive-through the scene with your own car, using the same path as the northbound striking vehicle; and
- A consultation with an collision reconstruction expert, who will assist with time and distance calculations, as well as determining the visibility of the driver at various points prior to the collision.

Always remain aware, however, of your ethical responsibilities. For example, if the driver in the above example, James Tyler Sullivan, is represented by counsel, the ethics rules bar you from speaking with him, either personally or through your investigator. However, you can take sworn declarations from the eyewitnesses. You will want to do this if they have additional details to offer that are not included in the police report.

Criminal Case Development

The strategic dimension of choosing between formal and informal discovery methods is not, in the main, a concern in criminal case development once charges have been filed. Generally, informal fact investigative methods are used to speak with witnesses. Access to documents, witness names, physical evidence, conviction records of witnesses, witnesses' statements, and such are guided by common law, statute, or court rule.

Investigations in the precharging phase are also generally informal in nature. Law enforcement officers interview witnesses, collect evidence, and so on. On the other hand, a witness can be summoned before the grand jury and compelled to testify under oath. As such, the grand jury could be considered to be a formal discovery device. Likewise, a warrant to search and seize evidence could be viewed as another formal means of gathering evidence.

III. PROGRESSION OF A CASE

This section will provide you with a rough sense of the flow of events within both a civil and a criminal case from inception through trial. To prepare properly for trial, you must understand the complete system and its different stages. Here we are not giving you a precise timeline or detailing typical time requirements dictated by court rules (say, the time allotted between the filing of a complaint and the date of a deposition). Compared to the complex, interrelated, and often fluid nature of the various aspects of the actual process, these summaries of the processes may appear mechanical and even a bit misleading. But it is our intention to provide you with relative reference points in time and stages of trial to aid you in understanding how a case progresses in your jurisdiction. Also, use this section from time to time throughout the course to review the case progression timeline.

A. A Civil Case

CIVIL CASE TIMELINE
INITIAL STAGE
A referral or some other communication is made in which the potential client contacts an attorney.
The attorney may decide to take the potential case.
Informal investigation of the facts takes place (interviewing witnesses, reading and obtaining documents from the client, other individuals, public records, and so on). For some of these, the attorney may hire an investigator.
After the informal investigation, the attorney may decide to contact the opposing adversary's attorney to explore a settlement. If unsuccessful, then proceed or refer the case out.
PLEADING
Attorney drafts, serves, and files pleadings: a complaint or petition for the plaintiff; an answer for a defending party.
Pretrial motions are filed, argued, and ruled on.

DISCOVERY

Depending on the jurisdiction, the court might require a pretrial or discovery case conference in which the schedule of the case is discussed, including discovery sequence, motions, and a tentative trial date.

The attorneys then begin formal discovery: send interrogatories, request production of documents, take depositions, or request for admissions, and so on.

MOTIONS AND NEGOTIATION

More motions may be filed and argued, such as a motion for summary judgment. Evidentiary motions may be heard (referred to as *in limine* motions).

Another pretrial/settlement conference may be held.

Throughout the pretrial process, the attorneys can discuss settlement.

ALTERNATIVE DISPUTE RESOLUTION

The case may go to arbitration or mediation.

TRIAL SEQUENCE

Trial sequence could begin with a waiver of a jury trial and the trial could be to the bench.

In the absence of a jury waiver, the trial begins with jury selection (voir dire).

Opening statements are made. The defense can reserve its opening statement until the beginning of the defense case.

The plaintiff's case-in-chief is argued; it is composed of direct examinations of witnesses, each followed by the defense cross-examining plaintiff's witness.

The defense case is argued; it too is composed of a series of direct and cross-examinations.

Both plaintiff and defense can orally make motions for judgment as a matter of law (directed verdict) after the opponent's opening statements, after an opponent's case-in-chief, or at the close of either side's case.

Assuming that the motion for judgment as a matter of law (directed verdict) is not granted, the court then informs the attorneys of the court's jury instructions that will be read to the jury; the attorneys, out of the presence of the jury, can take exception (object) to the court's determination of instructions and argue their points.

Closing arguments are heard. Jurisdictions differ in their order of closing arguments. Some courts instruct the jury and then allow closing arguments; other jurisdictions allow closing arguments and then instruct the jury. The plaintiff begins closing argument; then the defense argument is heard. Jurisdictions differ over whether plaintiff's lawyer will be permitted to make a rebuttal argument.

The jury retires to deliberate. The exhibits and, in some jurisdictions, the jury instructions are given to the jury to take to the jury room. Finally, there is a verdict regarding damages, or a hung jury if the jurors can not agree on a verdict.

Post-trial motions are made (motions for setting aside the verdict or altering the verdict, motions asking for a new trial or appealing, motions for additur, remittitur, bond for appeal).

APPEAL

After trial and post-trial motions, the losing party may appeal.

B.   A Criminal Case

CRIMINAL CASE TIMELINE

INITIAL STAGE

Ordinarily, for the defendant, a criminal case begins with an arrest. The arrest may be made on the scene by an observing police officer, or following an investigation that itself may be brief or lengthy, or after the convening of a secret grand jury.

Generally, it is also near the time of arrest that the defense attorney comes into the case, although sometimes an attorney arranges the initial surrender of a suspect.

However, in many cases the prosecution first learns of the case after the police have arrested the defendant and the case is submitted to the prosecution for a charging decision. In other cases, the case is submitted to the prosecutor for filing before arresting the defendant.

CHARGING

Generally, the prosecutor decides whether to file charges, and, if so, what to charge.

For misdemeanors, the prosecutor files a *complaint* in the lower trial court, usually called a district or municipal court, on which the defendant will face trial. Law enforcement may file a citation (traffic infraction, shoplifting) in a lower court.

For felonies, the procedure for bringing the charge varies among state and federal jurisdictions. In some jurisdictions, the prosecutor files a charging pleading called an *information* in the upper trial court, generally called the superior court, on which the defendant will face trial for the felony. In still others, the charge is stated in a complaint filed in the lower court, which then becomes the focus of a *preliminary hearing* where the prosecutor presents evidence to establish probable cause to believe the case should be bound over for trial in superior court.

In other jurisdictions, the prosecutor brings the case before a grand jury, which, if it finds the charges well founded, will return an *indictment*. Many jurisdictions, moreover, have available more than one of these charging procedures.

ARRAIGNMENT AND BAIL

The defendant is brought into court for arraignment. Defendant has a right to counsel at this proceeding. Technically, it is here that charges are read, a copy of the charging pleading is served on the defendant, and the defendant enters a plea.

A motion to reduce bail, if scheduled to be heard at this time, is argued.

DISCOVERY

After arraignment, both the prosecution and defense are engaged in informal discovery (witness interviews, disclosing witness statements) and formal discovery.

MOTIONS AND NEGOTIATION

Pretrial motions (suppression, change of venue, and so on) are filed and set for hearing.

The opposing counsel may file a response, and the motions are subsequently heard and ruled on by the court, often after a full evidentiary hearing with witnesses.

Additionally, prior to jury selection, evidentiary motions may be heard (referred to as in limine motions).

Negotiation may take place throughout the process, although defense counsel should first have conducted sufficient investigation and formal discovery to have a good grasp of the defendant's position.

If a disposition is reached, a formal plea hearing is set to put the plea on the record and to ensure that the defendant understands the rights the defendant is waiving and the consequences of the conviction.

After the guilty plea is entered, the court usually sets a date for sentencing and may order a study and presentence report by the probation department to assist in that task.

Sentencing follows.

TRIAL SEQUENCE

Trial sequence could begin with a waiver of a jury trial and the trial could be to the bench.

In the absence of a jury waiver, the trial begins with jury selection (voir dire).

Opening statements are made by the prosecutor and then the defense attorney. The defense may reserve its opening until the commencement of the prosecution case.

The prosecution case-in-chief is argued (direct examination by the prosecutor and cross-examination of witnesses by the defense).

The defense case-in-chief, if any, is argued (direct and cross-examination of witnesses); prosecution rebuttal, defense surrebuttal, if any.

Proposed jury instructions are submitted to the judge, with any arguments over instructions following; instructions are read to the jury. In some jurisdictions, instructions are given after closing argument.

Closing arguments are made (prosecution begins, defense follows; prosecution gets rebuttal, but in some jurisdictions, the prosecutor does not get to make a rebuttal argument).

The jury retires to deliberate. The exhibits and, in some jurisdictions, the jury instructions are given to the jury to take to the jury room.

Verdict or hung jury.

Post-trial motions are made (motion for new trial, bail on appeal, and so on).

Sentencing follows a guilty verdict.

APPEAL

After trial and post-trial motions, the defendant may appeal.

IV. INFORMAL FACT INVESTIGATION

A. The Investigator

For civil cases, no set pattern of fact investigation exists. The investigation could be assigned to a hired or an in-house investigator, a paralegal (think Erin Brockovich in the movie), or an attorney. The client, with your guidance, may act as the investigator, keeping notes and collecting records and physical evidence. In criminal cases, there is a pattern for fact investigation. Generally, law enforcement (the local police department, Federal Bureau of Investigation, sheriff's office, or similar group) gathers the evidence for the prosecution. The prosecutor may serve as an advisor or, in some instances, lead the investigation. Some prosecutors' offices have their own in-house investigators. Hired or in-house investigators perform investigations for defendants in criminal cases. Like their civil counterparts, there is no set pattern for criminal defense informal fact investigation.

B. The Expert: Consultant and Witness

The Fact-Development Diagram

An expert consultant can be crucial in case development by providing and/or directing you to fact and opinion evidence, in assisting with the formulation of the case theory, and in analyzing the other side's case theory. But how do you know whether an expert can assist in a particular case? As with other aspects of case development planning, the fact-development diagram is a good starting point.

In this regard, let's apply the diagram to the *Bicyclist-Crosswalk* case, see page 30. One tentative legal theory that you are pursuing is negligence by the motorist, James Tyler Sullivan.

ORGANIZING THE FACT INVESTIGATION

CASE FACTUAL INVESTIGATION DEVELOPMENT FOR PLAINTIFF

1. Elements	2. Factual Allegations	3. Evidence	4. Sources of Evidence	5. Investigation Method	6. Evidence Concerns
1. Duty	Marked crosswalk	Photos of scene	Police report	Client interview	Admissibility of witness opinions
2. Breach of Duty The motorist failed to yield the right-of-way to the bicyclist in the crosswalk, as required by the statute; did not stop to allow bicyclist to cross roadway in a marked crosswalk	Flashing yellow light

Bicyclist proceeded slowly

Bicyclist looked both ways

Bicyclist visible

Defendant was speeding
Defendant not paying attention (on cell phone) | Measurements

Witness statements | Possible expert consultation | Witness interviews

Possible expert consultation

Collision reconstruction technology | Possible allegation that client entered crosswalk when unsafe |

In the first column of the diagram, you list the elements of that claim for relief. As an illustration, we will focus on the element of duty as set out in the motor vehicle code: that the defendant operator of the approaching vehicle shall stop and remain stopped to allow a bicyclist to cross the roadway within a marked crosswalk when the bicycle is on or within one lane of a half of the roadway on which the vehicle is traveling, and the bicyclist entered the crosswalk at a time it was safe to do so. The factual assertion is this:

> Plaintiff Litonya Barefoot, the bicyclist, was in the crosswalk and that the oncoming car failed to yield the right-of-way; that the plaintiff left the curb and entered the crosswalk at a time when it was safe to do so, when it was possible for an oncoming driver to stop. The defendant motorist should have seen the bicyclist in sufficient time to stop and avoid the collision.

To support this assertion, we have Ms. Barefoot's story that she was in a marked crosswalk with a flashing yellow light overhead at a time it was safe to cross, and that she looked both ways before entering the crosswalk and proceeded slowly. Suddenly she saw defendant Sullivan's Honda Civic coming at her at a high rate of speed. There was no way to avoid being hit by defendant's car at that point. All this is reflected in the first two columns of the preceding fact-development diagram.

Using your common sense and the information you have acquired to date, you realize that other allegations bearing on the elements of duty and breach might be possibilities. For instance, you may consider adding the following allegations to duty and breach: As shown by the visibility photograph on page 31, taken by a bystander at the moment prior to the accident, exiting a nearby parking lot was a van that partially obscured the vision of the northbound traffic on 12th Avenue, and the defendant driver must have been inattentive to traffic blocking his view of the crosswalk. Ms. Barefoot is not qualified as an expert to express an opinion, for example, on whether the position at which the van was stopped had indeed obscured the defendant motorist's visibility of the bicyclist at the time. You would probably conclude that an expert, conducting motion and impact tests, may be able to render an opinion that a van had obstructed the defendant's view of the crosswalk. An expert could also show you problems with your case (the bicyclist should have seen that if she was in the crosswalk, she would not be visible to a motorist in time for the motorist to stop). At this juncture in the case development, you might benefit from an expert with whom you can consult.

Consultant Analysis

If a consulting expert is hired only for preparation of litigation, her opinion and any information she generates are likely to be work product privileged. An expert retained to testify at trial must be disclosed during discovery, and this expert's information is not privileged. A consulting expert also may later become a designated expert for trial.

A consulting expert may first provide information on issues such as these:

- What fields of expertise apply?
- What are the issues to which an expert could speak?

For example, in the *Bicyclist-Crosswalk* case, a collision reconstructionist can recreate the scene prior to and at the time of the collision to provide time and distance estimates that will allow you to state when the motorist should have seen the bicyclist, when he should have applied his brakes, and whether that would have allowed him to avoid the collision. The collision reconstruction expert can also provide an opinion as to speed and whether the view of the crosswalk was obstructed creating an unsafe condition. The consulting expert could also advise on these questions:

- Who are the experts qualified to provide testimony in these fields?
- What evidence and sources of evidence should you seek through your informal investigation and the formal discovery process?
- What evidentiary concerns exist? (Is the chosen expert qualified? Is there a scientific basis for the opinion?)
- What are the strengths and weaknesses in the defense case theory, including potential defense expert testimony?

C.   Should You Retain an Expert?

You have now determined that you could use an expert and have even focused on the field of expertise required. All that, however, does not mean that you will in fact hire an expert. The next stage is a process of elimination. Matters coming into play at this stage include, among others: economic factors, the lack of any available scientific technique, an absence of evidence, and the existence of a better approach.

Economic Factors

Experts can be expensive, and the cost may be prohibitive. While the prosecutor in a homicide case may be able to obtain the services of publicly funded crime laboratory experts, private counsel generally does not have this advantage. Private counsel must consider expense funds at every stage beginning with case development, when an expert may provide valuable advice and technical information; right through expert investigation, when scientific testing, for example, might be needed; and, ultimately, to expert trial testimony.

You need to consider whether you can justify the expense of employing an expert's services. You may decide not to use an expert because in your judgment, perhaps after consultation with an expert or after self-education on the technical aspects, the expert does not support your legal theory, or is not likely to produce the results you want, or is just not worth the expense. Of course, if expense in relationship to the valuation of the case is problematic, you might consider more creative options. Sometimes a witness to the event can also serve as a cost-free expert. For example, in the *Bicyclist-Crosswalk* case, consider using the investigating police officer as your expert since the officer will support your legal theory.

Scientific Techniques Unavailable

Another factor that can help determine if you will use an expert in a case investigation is whether some scientific technique exists that is capable of producing useful information for your case. For instance, your consulting expert could advise you that the type of testing that you speculated would be useful is not an option because the scientific technique has not been perfected. In other words, the technique is not commonly accepted as reliable in the scientific community and therefore may be inadmissible at trial. You will need to determine what evidentiary test your jurisdiction employs to make such a methodological reliability analysis—the *Frye* or the *Daubert* test—and comply with the requirements. See Chapter 11 on experts, in the *Trial Advocacy* text.

Absence of Evidence

The absence of any evidence to be tested would block pursuing expert investigation and testimony. For example, while it might seem inconceivable that critical evidence might be unavailable for testing, it could turn out that the intersection has been significantly altered since the collision.

A Better Approach

You may decide that using other evidence such as lay testimony, exhibits, or even argument in lieu of expert testimony is tactically a better approach. For example, you could conclude that the collision reconstructionist's testimony would be weak and that you would be better off presenting what happened through Ms. Barefoot's testimony and the investigating officer's testimony, arguing to a jury that it is common sense to draw a conclusion that an experienced bicyclist such as Litonya Barefoot would not have entered the crosswalk unless it was safe to do so. On the other hand, if there are too many conflicting eye witnesses statements, this argument may not be convincing.

D. Selecting an Expert

Assuming that after this process of elimination you still want an expert consultant, you have arrived at the point when you will need to choose a specific expert. Initially, you should be aware that an expert may be selected for you without your direct involvement. In the *Bicyclist-Crosswalk* case, the investigating officer, Kim Jarvis, may have decided that the defendant Sullivan was speeding and issued a citation for speeding. In this instance, it is likely that you will be calling the investigating officer as your expert witness. Similar circumstances occur with medical experts, so that the plaintiff's attorney might call the treating doctor as the medical expert in the case.

In the usual situation, however, you will select the expert yourself. We propose a decision-making process for the selection of a specific expert that involves an analysis of three considerations: (1) conclusions compatible with your case theory, (2) skills of the expert, and (3) practical problems.

1. Conclusions Compatible with Your Case Theory

Civil and Criminal Case Considerations

Analysis of whether to choose a particular person as an expert begins at the beginning—your case theory. Underpinning your decision to select the person as your expert is the premise that the expert will provide testimony helpful in proving your case theory or in attacking your opponent's case theory. Therefore, a primary consideration might be whether the person would make investigative findings and provide helpful testimony.

That does not mean that you seek out an expert who simply says whatever you want to hear. Quite the contrary. In the first place, in every aspect of your planning and preparation, you want to know about possible problems with proving your case theory. The domain of expertise is no exception. For example, as plaintiff's counsel in our *Bicyclist-Crosswalk* case, you want a knowledgeable expert who will candidly tell you whether the motorist had sufficient time and distance to avoid the collision. Rather than bulling ahead toward an inevitably disastrous trial, you now can consider options such as developing a new case theory that can withstand expert scrutiny, or seeking quick settlement, or advising the client to stop pursuing the lawsuit and avoid putting good money after bad.

In the second place, one of the worst mistakes an attorney can make with an expert is to try to push the expert into an opinion beyond what the person's expertise can support. Not only does this create professional discomfort for the expert, it also is likely to result in transforming helpful evidence into harmful evidence. Imagine that a collision reconstructionist expert tells you that "while I cannot say absolutely that the speed of the motorist caused the collision, I can say unequivocally that it is in no way inconsistent with having resulted in the collision." Of course, you would like the expert to say "absolutely caused," but that's not what her expertise can support. So take what she is giving you, run with it, and look to amass enough nonexpert evidence corroborating your causation theory such that, in combination with the expert's opinion of "consistency," you will get past any summary judgment motion and are well on your way to settlement or to a jury. On the other hand, if you try to force the expert away from "is in no way inconsistent with having resulted" to "absolutely caused," the expert likely will present herself as uncomfortable and unsure, and will probably get hammered by opposing counsel in a deposition and at trial. You will have not only lost the helpful evidence the expert had to offer, but also harmed your entire case by showing the fact finder that you are willing to present weak, noncredible evidence.

Additional Considerations in Criminal Cases

Prosecutor

Think about this desire for an expert who can support your case theory in the criminal context. Assume that you are the prosecutor assigned to a homicide case and that it is your job to oversee case development. Assume for the moment you want to establish that the suspect, the boyfriend, committed the crime. Let's look at the *Bite-Mark* case.

The *Bite-Mark* Case

Story

A jogger in Laurelhurst Park spotted Tamica Roy's dead body in a wooded area next to the jogging path. During the autopsy, the medical examiner observed what appeared to be a bite mark on the victim's left shoulder. The night before Ms. Roy's body was discovered, a neighbor overheard a loud quarrel in the apartment that Ms. Roy shared with her boyfriend, Brandon Robinson.

A forensic odontologist could examine Ms. Roy's body, photograph the marks, and take impressions. The odontologist could then compare photographs and impressions of the suspect's teeth with the photographs and impressions of the marks, and ultimately reach conclusions regarding whether Mr. Robinson's teeth made the bite marks.

One of the most infamous cases involving bite-mark testimony was in obtaining the conviction of the serial killer, Ted Bundy, when a bite mark on the victim's buttock was matched to dental impressions of Bundy's teeth. Katherine Ramsland, *The Most Famous Bite*, TruTV Crime Library, *http://www.crimelibrary.com/forensics/bitemarks/* (Time Warner Co., 2007).

In deciding whether to enlist a particular odontologist, you might want a person who is likely to investigate and come to the conclusion that Mr. Robinson's teeth made the bite marks. You recognize the realistic possibility that scientific investigation may lead to findings that are either inconclusive or that exclude the suspect as the person who left the marks. In the latter situation, the scientific investigation would produce exculpatory evidence that either would justly lead to the exoneration of innocent Mr. Robinson or, if the prosecution believed under the circumstances that there still existed sufficient evidence of guilt, would have to be disclosed to the defense.

If your only obligation as a prosecutor were to prove the criminal charge, and not as it is to seek justice, you would think only about finding a bite-mark expert who could credibly tell you what you wanted to hear, tempered by the previous discussion of the dangers of trying to force the expert to say more than his expertise can support. Somewhat different is a more cynical viewpoint that an expert is a commodity to be shopped for. This viewpoint certainly may be offensive to all those who would hope that scientific testing and expert opinion would be objective and not subject to outside influences such as who hired the expert. Realistically, however, some experts may be influenced. Also, science is not cut-and-dried. Reasonable people can differ, situations can be ambiguous, and, especially in "soft" sciences like those studying human behavior, an expert who routinely works with attorneys and who adopts an ends-means perspective can plausibly support a position that is 180 degrees from that of an opponent's expert.

Now stand back from what we've been doing. While the prosecutor may want to find the expert who will make favorable findings, again, blind attachment to such an approach has intrinsic perils. Paramount is the danger that this expert is merely a hired gun who will distort any factual situation to reach the result desired by the party who employed her. This carries two problems. A talented forensic faker can demean the justice system as well as the legal profession, no matter what the verdict might be. On a more practical level, the distortion may be exposed at trial. In fact, any evidence during the trial that the expert's work has been influenced by an excessive fee arrangement, bias toward a party, or personal inclination may greatly diminish the expert's testimony and possibly damage the proponent's entire case.

As the prosecutor, you have an ethical obligation that overrides any tendency you might have to select a biased expert. Your duty is to do justice, not just to convict. Mindful of this principle, you should decide to choose the expert based on the person's expertise in the field, as well as the person's investigative and forensic skills.

Defense Counsel

Now consider the decision-making processes of defense counsel in the same criminal case. Your responsibility as defense counsel is to ensure that Mr. Robinson, who is constitutionally guaranteed competent representation, receives the best defense ethically possible. That does not involve responsibility to seek potentially damaging information. Therefore, you as defense counsel would want to choose the expert who would render a favorable finding. For example, in the *Bite-Mark* case, you would want an expert who would be likely to find that the marks on the body were not bite marks or, if they were bite marks, either exclude Mr. Robinson or were inconclusive. You could consider the prior performance and other factors (the expert has customarily testified for the defense) in deciding whether to employ the person. However, like the prosecutor, you would be concerned about hiring a person who might be vulnerable to being exposed as having a bias or interest, or who cannot be trusted to proceed forthrightly and honestly.

2. Skills of the Expert

One approach to choosing a specific expert is to evaluate the characteristics of the possible experts against a profile of the ideal expert witness. While you may not find the perfect expert witness, the profile will allow you to weigh the strengths and weaknesses of potential experts. Think about the characteristics of the ideal expert witness. Commonly, an expert will perform essentially two functions: one as investigator and another as witness. The person's abilities in these areas should be major considerations.

The Expert as an Investigator

An ideal expert would be a highly competent investigator and recognizable as an expert in the field. Preferably, the investigation would personally involve the expert during evidence-gathering. The expert would carefully examine all evidence, perform appropriate scientific tests, and prepare or suggest for preparation demonstrative evidence that would be helpful in illustrating the expert's testimony (photographs, models). Implicitly, this means that the expert should be someone with whom you can work.

Qualified Under Evidence Rules

Now consider the profile of the ideal expert witness from the perspective of the expert's role as a witness. First, there are issues of admissibility to be determined by the court. Thus, the expert must be able to qualify under the appropriate state or federal evidence, rule such as Federal Rule of Evidence 702, that they can impart helpful specialized or technical knowledge to the jury based on their "knowledge, skill, training, or experience." In assessing their expertise, be certain to match their specific expertise with the scope of the testimony you desire. In other words, an expert cardiologist testifying about a heart attack precipitated by a painful beating may be successfully objected to if she attempts to go too deeply into orthopedic injuries. Part of qualifications might also include the very legitimacy of the proposed expertise (such as polygraphy) or the particular methodology used by the expert, such as whether an epidemiologist used proper data and studies. In some states, the court will decide this latter question, at least as to the novel scientific methods, based on the so-called *Frye* standard (whether the area of expertise or particular methodology is "generally accepted in the scientific community"); while in other states and all federal courts, the judge will apply the *Daubert* standard ("reliable methodology"), both of which are discussed in the *Trial Advocacy* text, Chapter 11 on experts.

Qualified in the Eyes of the Jury

Even assuming the expert's testimony is admissible under evidence rules, an attorney must consider how persuasive the expert will be in convincing the jury. An expert's qualifications, just discussed as a legal requirement, are obviously also a significant factor in the expert's persuasiveness, especially if they are particularly impressive or better than the qualifications of an expert called by the opposing party. The expert's qualifications will also determine the permissible scope of the expert's testimony. For example, a police officer who, because of training and experience, qualifies to give an opinion about an collision from skid-mark evidence may not be qualified to estimate speeds by applying principles of physics to car damage.

Impartiality and Objectivity

The ideal expert is also a person the jury will perceive as impartial and objective. Information about the expert that you might consider in deciding whether the person probably will project these qualities includes whether the witness testified significantly more often for one side in lawsuits than the other (the witness is employed by the state crime laboratory and, unsurprisingly, always testifies for the prosecution). Or, whether the person has a financial interest in the case (a major portion of their income comes from forensic testimony, giving them an incentive to obtain successful results for those who hired them in order to obtain future business). Additionally, whether the expert usually finds the same facts or comes to the same conclusions; whether an employment bias exists (the expert testifies in favor of the party who has hired her); and whether personal or professional bias is a factor (the expert adheres to a particular theory over which there is a dispute).

Communications Skills

Assess what your expert's potential charisma rating is. Jurors look to more than the resume-type qualifications that tend to impress many lawyers. Your adversary will also recognize any deficiencies in your expert's charisma, and that will affect settlement in a civil or a plea bargain in a criminal case. The expert with the best resume does not necessarily win a case. While jurors certainly expect an expert witness to be knowledgeable, the expert's attitude and communications skills are far more important in determining credibility. A know-it-all expert with a superior condescending attitude who speaks in pedantic jargon-laden phrases will be quickly rejected. The same will be the result for a prickly, defensive expert who is combative and hostile on cross-examination. Think of your favorite teacher in school. What made you like and respect him so much? The same principle applies to expert witnesses in court. Jurors like experts who are helpful and accessible, make eye contact and engage them. It also helps if the expert has warmth, enthusiasm for the subject, and a sense of humor. Like your favorite teacher in school, the best experts also know how to illustrate scientific or technical principles by using accessible analogies or appealing to the visual sense of jurors. For example, in the *Bicyclist-Crosswalk* case, you should be on the lookout for a collision reconstruction expert who has taught courses to law enforcement officers and who has access to the variety of government-funded studies on bicycle-motorist collisions at crosswalks.

3. Practical Problems

Frequently encountered practical problems facing an attorney trying to choose an expert include how to locate a suitable expert, how to compensate the expert, and how many experts to employ.

Locating Experts

A reliable way to find a suitable expert who most closely matches the expert witness profile is to consult with lawyers, experts, and others whose judgment is trusted and who have firsthand knowledge of the expert's ability. The Internet and legal databases provide an excellent way to locate experts in every field. The lawyer grapevine is one of the most commonly used and effective ways of locating good experts. For example, in the *Bicyclist-Crosswalk* case, you could look for other reported verdicts and settlements in similar cases in your jurisdiction. These will list not only the type of case and the name of the lawyer, but also the experts used. If you call the lawyer, you will get an in-depth report of how well the particular expert worked. Many lawyer organizations also have a computer listserv where members share information. You could send out an e-mail asking for suggestions on experts (remembering, of course, not to divulge any sensitive information about your case; e-mail communications are not protected by the attorney-client privilege and do not fall under professional rules of confidentiality). In addition, you may resort to directories of forensic evidence experts, such as *The Forensic Science Directory* (National Forensic Center). Also, jury verdicts reported in Westlaw and LEXIS-NEXIS databases and attorney professional publications bar association materials, and news reports may contain information about experts.

Compensation

You also need to be concerned about compensation of the expert witness. Forensic experts tend to be relatively expensive, as many others in the same field do not wish to get involved in the stresses and inconveniences of testifying. Accordingly, experts who do agree to consult in cases typically expect to receive a premium for the time and trouble involved in doing forensic work.

In civil cases, economics plays a major role in hiring an expert because rarely will courts appoint experts. Generally, expert witness fees in civil cases are high and may be cost prohibitive, depending on the value of the case. Expert fees may contain provision for travel, hotels, and other accommodations. Carefully weigh the costs and benefits of an expert to your case. Determining the appropriate fee, the hourly rate, and the cost reimbursements may be difficult and may require consultation with other attorneys or other sources.

As previously mentioned, government attorneys may be provided with no-cost services from a publicly funded state or local crime laboratory or be able to call on the services of the Federal Bureau of Investigation Crime Laboratory for assistance. Beyond that, both a prosecutor and an indigent defendant may be able to request a court-appointed expert and have the court order payment from either a state or local budget.

If an expert made observations and reached conclusions, say, as a treating physician, before becoming a court-appointed expert, local law may provide that the person may be subpoenaed and required to testify for only the usual fee paid to a lay witness. While compelling testimony without an expert fee might be economical, you may well be faced with a recalcitrant witness.

Number of Experts

Finally, you must decide on the number of expert witnesses to employ. First, while you may want to call several experts to speak on a single issue so that each, in effect, corroborates the other and the jury does not get the sense that only one person shares this expert opinion, this tactic carries with it some possible problems. Multiple expert witnesses in the same field might render contradictory or somewhat inconsistent findings or opinions, or rely on different bases for their opinions, and therefore undermine each other's credibility.

Second, while experts testifying about different issues are generally not going to contradict each other, other concerns still exist. A case inundated with expert witnesses, techniques, and jargon may become confusing. A frequent complaint from jurors is that lawyers go over and over the same material. Jurors in our media-centric age are sophisticated consumers of information—they get the point very quickly and tend to prefer economy and simplicity. Saturation bombing of redundant information through a parade of experts quickly causes resentment; jurors may feel that it insults their intelligence. To the extent your case appears to center on expert testimony, you may lose the genuine underlying emotions and equities in your case, replacing them with a series of academic questions answered by experts, and may precipitate a battle of experts in which the jurors will flip a coin between your experts and your opponent's.

E.   Exhibits

Consider the location, inspection, and preservation of potential exhibits. In a criminal case, law enforcement has set procedures for evidence collection, labeling and preserving it in an evidence room until trial. For example, in the *Bite-Mark* case, the pathologist or a detective would have photographed the bite marks on Ms. Roy's body. The impressions of Mr. Robinson's teeth would have been packaged, given an evidence label and number, and stored in the evidence room of the police department. The chain of custody for the evidence would be carefully maintained.

The same principles apply to civil case evidence collection and preservation. Remember that in the *Bicyclist-Crosswalk* case, we suggested that the intersection of the crash with the passage of time might conceivably be altered. What should the lawyer do to prepare for this possibility? As soon as the attorney learns about the case, the lawyer should visit the scene of the crash, direct that it be photographed and/or videotaped, and make a timely decision about hiring an expert such as a collision reconstructionist.

The attorney also needs to establish a system of labeling and storing the evidence from the intersection and the related expert reports so that witnesses will later be able to effectively use this evidence to testify about the scene as it was when the crash occurred. None of this would be difficult to do in the *Bicyclist-Crosswalk* case. In contrast, such organization, storage, and preservation would be significantly more difficult with fungible physical evidence, such as white powder, which needs to be placed in a container, sealed, labeled, and stored in a place protected from outside tampering. Special consideration must be given to the preservation of organic material, such as perishable products or human or animal components. Proper preservation of vital evidence is critical to success at trial.

Exhibits are critical to persuasive advocacy. Chapter 8 in the *Trial Advocacy* text is specifically devoted to exhibits and the visual trial.

V.   MANAGING THE CASE

Getting ready for trial can be demanding work. As you prepare and develop your case, it may seem at times as if you face an oncoming avalanche of information—thousands of pages of records and reports, a mass of e-mails and other electronically stored information, deposition transcripts and videos, correspondence, and much more. You will need to organize and manage this burgeoning information. Your management system should file the information in an orderly fashion so you can easily search for and retrieve what you want when you want it. That system should facilitate a privilege review and production of discovery. The management system should guarantee that

you perform all the necessary tasks to prepare for trial, such as witness inter-
viewing, subpoenaing the witnesses, and so on.

In trial, the management system should enable you to quickly locate,
retrieve, and effectively display the information you want to show the jury.
The system should facilitate how you perform each phase of trial from arguing motions, engaging in jury selection, making an opening statement on
through to delivering closing argument. This section is devoted to management systems that will help you accomplish these goals. We provide a comprehensive trial preparation checklist. It lists what needs to be done during
trial preparation and refers you to other parts of the book where we explore
in detail particular tasks. For instance, we offer a summary list of what needs
to be done to prepare for jury selection and then refer you to pages in the
jury selection chapter where you can find an in-depth discussion of how to
manage information needed for voir dire.

A. Electronic Case Management

Software is available to manage the information onslaught that can be part
of your pretrial litigation. This software is designed to do the following tasks,
among others:

- Receive and store the information in a database;
- Sort the information by categories, such as chronology, people, events,
  and issues;
- Search the database to locate and retrieve information;
- Facilitate case analysis by sorting and other analytical functions;
- Annotate documents and images in the database;
- Redact objectionable portions of a transcript;
- Manage transcripts; and
- Conduct a privilege review and produce discovery.

CASE MANAGEMENT AND TRIAL PRESENTATION SOFTWARE

The following lists several case management and trial presentation software:

- **Concordance** from Dataflight Software, Inc.—case management software
  that accommodates large cases (*http://www.dataflight.com*)

continues ▶

> - **CaseMap** from CaseSoft—case management and analysis software (*http://www.casesoft.com*)
> - **Summation** from CT Summation—case management and trial presentation software (*http://www.summation.com*)
> - **Visionary** from Visionary Legal Technologies—case management and trial presentation software (*http://www.visionarylegaltechnologies.com*)
> - **PowerPoint** from Microsoft Corp.—trial presentation software (*http://www.office.microsoft.com*)
> - **TrialDirector** from inData, Corp.—trial presentation software (*http://www.indatacorp.com*)
> - **Sanction** from Verdict Systems—trial presentation software (*http://www.verdictsystems.com*)
> - **TrialPro** from IDEA, Inc.—trial presentation software (*http://www.trialpro.com*)

To truly grasp what this technology offers, you need to experience it. Most of the software mentioned offer a trial period to test the product and some offer Web seminars that walk you through the use of the software. The following overview of electronic management software provides a rudimentary guide about how the software operates and, more important, what this software can do for you in pretrial litigation and trial.

Database

The lawyer, paralegal, and/or outside litigation support service, such as Litigation Abstract, Inc. or Visionary Legal Technology, create the electronic management system's database. Documents and images, such as a photographic exhibit, are scanned into the system. Electronic documents, such as transcripts of depositions, e-mails, pleadings, and other electronic information, are coded, numbered, and loaded into the system. Initially, this information may be entered into a database, such as Microsoft's Access, and later imported into the case management software. Widely used case management software includes Concordance, Summation, and CaseMap.

Search and Retrieval

A feature common to case management software is the ability to search for, locate, and retrieve what is needed from a mass of information. Using words, topics, or phrases, the software rapidly locates the sought information. For example, if you are planning to depose a witness, you can search for the witness's name in all the database information including prior testimony, inner-office memoranda, e-mails, correspondence, and so on.

Case Analysis

Electronic case management software provides a case organization and analysis tool somewhat like the fact-development diagram discussed earlier in this chapter. However, the electronic tool is more efficient and more effective.

CaseMap is an example of what computer technology can do for case organization and analysis. CaseMap provides a spreadsheet that links the essentials of a case: facts, objects (people, places), issues, questions (things the lawyer is searching for), and legal research. As the case is developed, new information, such as a new witness's name, is added to the spreadsheet. The program also has a thinking tool that permits the user to evaluate the information (a positive rating for a witness). The software links the spreadsheet's information so that with a double click all information relating to a particular person can be called up. CaseMap also exports information to TimeMap, a software program that creates timelines of events.

During case preparation, you can annotate and flag information for later retrieval. For example, Summation has a feature that allows the user to highlight, like a yellow highlighter, "Hotfacts" that can be called up later from the database. Another example of how the software can aid in analysis is Summation's transcript digest feature by which the lawyer highlights portions of the deposition transcript, types in desired annotations, and transfers the highlighted and annotated transcript excerpts to a digest for retrieval.

Hosting the Database

Electronic case management allows the database to be accessed over the Internet. Therefore, for instance, multiple law firms working on a products liability case could share information online. Or an expert could review case information online.

Discovery

With electronic management software such as Concordance, the lawyer can do a privilege review, redact where necessary, and then produce discovery. The software provides production numbers and tracks production of discovery. (Bates numbers, production numbers that are hand-stamped onto documents, generally have been replaced by electronic technology tools serving the same purpose.)

Pretrial, Trial, and Settlement Presentations

For trial, alternative dispute resolution, or settlement conferences, the images and documents stored in the electronic management software may need to be transferred to trial presentation software—TrialDirector, Sanction, Visionary, TrialPro, or PowerPoint. This presentation software is used to display the images, such as photographs, documents, or portions of a deposition transcript, to the opposing side (for negotiation purposes) or to the fact finder. See Chapter 8 in the *Trial Advocacy* text, which is devoted to visuals and the use of presentation software.

B.   Trial System

You need to be organized before trial. Eventually you will settle on a trial organizational system that works best for you. It may be primarily electronic in nature or it may be paper-based, using trial notebooks, accordion files, file drawers, or some combination of these systems. Whatever trial system you adopt, to be effective, it must be orderly and enable you to store information easily and to retrieve it quickly. The following is a checklist for your trial system, whether it is electronic or paper based. If you adopt the trial notebooks approach, you could use the dividers in a three-ring binder notebook for trial subdivisions. With folders kept in an expanding file, you could label the tabs on the folders with the subdivision labels. If using an electronic system, the subdivisions could serve as folder labels on your computer.

 TRIAL SYSTEM SUBDIVISIONS

Consider these subdivisions for your trial system, whether it is electronic or paper based:

- Journal;
- Thinking;
- Case Summary Sheet;
- Motions, Orders, Stipulations, and Trial Brief;
- Jury Selection;

- Opening Statement;
- Witnesses;
- Direct Examination;
- Cross-Examination;
- Exhibits and Trial Visuals;
- Jury Instructions;
- Closing Argument;
- Pleadings;
- Discovery; and
- To-Do List.

Which trial system you adopt depends on your comfort level with the system. Some trial lawyers are comfortable with an electronic management system (others are not) and financial resources. Like so many trial lawyers, you probably will arrive at a system after trial and error with different methods.

Journal

Your organizational system should include a chronological case journal of significant things that you do regarding the case. For example: "5/23/XX — Received telephone call from plaintiff's counsel, Alfred Riggio, and scheduled a meeting on 6/28/XX at his office." However it is stored, electronically or on paper, it should be recorded with the case file, not just in a daily planner. The journal can come in handy in recalling dates and sometimes help you prove an event took place. For example, the judge might inquire into whether you conferred with opposing counsel before bringing a motion.

Thinking File

You're commuting to work, and flash, you get an insight for your closing argument. Brilliant. In the middle of the night, you get the idea for that case theme that you have been searching for. Again, brilliant. A day or a week later, and you are struggling to remember those brilliant thoughts. Brilliant and forgotten because they were not written down.

At the outset of any case, open electronic and/or paper files for your thoughts. Then, record your brainstorms as they come to you. The notes will prove invaluable later as you plan to perform the particular pretrial or trial activity. Normally, at the outset of any case, as with any new endeavor, the mind will offer a wealth of thoughts, and those fresh ideas are some of the best. In particular, you should create thinking files on these topics:

- Case theories and themes,
- Settlement,
- Demonstrative evidence,
- Jury selection,
- Opening statement,
- Cross-examination, and
- Closing argument.

The computer is a particularly useful place to record your thoughts. As you open a case, just create an "Ideas" folder (or whatever label you wish to give the folder) and within this folder create subfolders labeled along the lines of the topics listed above. If the idea comes to you when you are at the computer, just type it in. Or, if you are away from the computer and do not use or have access to a PDA when the idea comes to you, scribble notes on whatever is available and then enter it in the computer at the next available opportunity.

Case Summary Sheet

One more tool for your use: the Case Summary Sheet. We suggest that the basic information about the case be reduced to one piece of paper that is readily accessible during pretrial and trial. A lawyer will, in the press of a heavy caseload, eventually discover that moment when vital information slips away from the mind, such as the location of the collision or the client's name. The Case Summary Chart gives the trial lawyer a safety net.

CASE SUMMARY
CASE CAPTION: CLIENT'S NAME: OTHER PARTIES' NAME: CLAIM(S) WITH DATE(S): TIME(S) AND LOCATION(S): THUMBNAIL CASE DESCRIPTION:

Motions, Orders, Trial Brief, Stipulations, and Pocket Briefs

Motions, Orders, Trial Brief, and Stipulations

If the motion has been served and filed, the trial system will contain a copy of the motion and an order if it has been ruled on. Each motion and order will be separately tabbed by subject, "Motion in limine—Bifurcation." Likewise, stipulations can be filed under a separate subdivision.

Pocket Briefs

A pocket brief (so-called because you figuratively keep it in your pocket until needed), is a brief on an evidentiary issue that may come up during trial, that has not been served or filed. It is best to keep a pocket brief in a file so that when the time comes you can hand it to the court and opposing counsel. In the file, you will have the original that the court clerk can file, as well as copies to serve on opposing counsel and to provide the judge.

Argument Notes

We also prefer the technique of reducing motion arguments to outline notes and then placing those notes on the inside of a manila folder. This allows you to not only maintain eye contact with the judge and not read your argument but also appear professional and organized.

Jury Selection

When it comes to organization, jury selection is particularly demanding if the trial lawyer is actively involved in the questioning. You do not want paper or other obstacles to your communication with prospective jurors, and yet you need to work with and manage paper.

Jury Binder

We prefer a separate jury selection binder that can be used for trial. The contents of the binder could include, among other things: law relevant to jury selection (statutes and court rules on challenges for cause and peremptory challenges); your agenda for jury selection; jury selection notes or questions grouped by subject areas to be asked during jury selection; good juror and bad juror profiles; list of witnesses with names, addresses, and occupations. You would include a Jury Seating Chart and a Challenges Chart, see Chapter 6, *Trial Advocacy* text, pages 171 and 172.

Opening Statement and Closing Argument

The subparts of these two segments of trial can be organized in a similar fashion. Create one subdivision for opening statement and another for closing argument, and then create the following subsections for each.

Brilliant Ideas

You want a place in the trial system where you can write down your ideas as they come to you during trial preparation. Once again, you want to preserve your thoughts by noting them.

Preparing Opening and Closing

Although some believe that trial lawyers should not write their opening statements or closing arguments because they then will tend to read instead of speak them, we disagree. Among the reasons for writing opening and closing is that the process will force the trial lawyer to select persuasive language and to carefully structure the opening and closing. Both are speeches, and speeches should be meticulously drafted. The subdivisions for opening would contain the written opening and, even more important, the brief outline with keywords that the lawyer can remove from the file or notebook and use during the opening or closing. Having only the outline during opening or closing prevents the trial lawyer from reading. Ideally, in fact, trial counsel will never look at a note but speak directly to jurors throughout his opening and closing.

Witnesses

Witness Lists

This trial system subdivision should contain a witness list with all contact information for each witness, including name, home and business addresses, and phone numbers; relatives or other people who can be contacted to locate the witness if necessary; and an indication that the witness has been subpoenaed. Also, you should create another witness list without contact information on it. The one with contact information is most useful if it is alphabetical so you can easily locate the witness. Make the list into a document with the case caption and the title, such as "Plaintiff's List of Witnesses." This list can be provided to the judge and opposing counsel. The judge can read the list to the prospective jurors and inquire if any of them recognize the witnesses.

Order of Witnesses

While the witness list with contact information and the one given to the judge can have any order you wish, you must develop an order-of-witness list in which you will call witnesses. The most common way to arrange the order of your witnesses for your case-in-chief is to start with a strong witness and end with a strong witness and bury the weaker ones in the middle, keeping in mind the desire to present as coherent a narrative as possible.

Direct Examination Outline or Questions

We suggest writing the questions. Later, you can outline, list bullet points, or keep writing the questions. Important questions, such as a question to elicit an expert's opinion, should be written out even by experienced trial lawyers. If you have written the full question, the challenge is to deliver it naturally so the direct is like an unscripted conversation. A method for preparing notes is to draw a line down the center of a page of lined paper and write the questions on the left side for direct or cross-examination. During direct, you can use the right side to jot notes of significant answers. Put notations in the margins to indicate the legal authority supporting admission of the evidence if there is any question about it. Also, in appropriate places in your notes, indicate the exhibits you wish to introduce or use to illustrate the points you need to present.

Direct examination notes can be filed in a notebook or in a folder or another storage place that can be in hand as you question the witness. We prefer to put them in a folder with fasteners (those two metal strips that stick out at the top) that go through holes at the top of the paper. You can put your questions or outline on the right side of the file and on the left side put the witness's prior statements, checklist of essential facts, and an exhibits' list for that witness. This folder is easier to work with than a bulky notebook, and you can flip the pages over the top of the folder as you finish a page.

Prior Statements and Depositions

Depositions and witness prior statements can be stored in notebooks and/
or in a computer. Either way, they must be easily accessible and retriev-
able if need be. As mentioned earlier, computer software enables the user
to quickly locate and retrieve necessary documents. If the trial lawyer is not
using computer software, prior statements can be indexed with keywords
and phrases so that the lawyer can access the pertinent part of the deposition or statement when needed. Page references can be noted in the margin
of the direct examination questions or outline.

Cross-Examination Outline or Questions

The methods for storing notes for cross-examination questions are the same
as those for direct examination, but the format differs. Write the title for the
argument you will make at the end of the case ("Witness Is Biased"). Number
each page relating to that subject. When you start a new topic, start with page
1. Next, draw a line down the middle of the page. On the left side, write short
statements of fact. The right column is available to write references to the file
(such as a statement in witness's deposition or e-mail) in case the witness
does not provide the desired answer and you need to promptly access your
proof. Also, the right column can be used to record and highlight the witness's
notable answers.

Exhibits and Trial Visuals

Exhibit List

An exhibit list is the place where you keep track of action taken with your
and the other side's exhibits. An exhibit list contains information about
exhibits offered and the disposition of them. Were they admitted? Denied?
Why? While this list can be stored in a file, notebook, or computer, we prefer
an exhibit file with fasteners at the top because it is handy and can be easily
carried around in the courtroom when working with exhibits.

The Exhibits

How you manage an exhibit naturally depends on the nature of the exhibit.
The trial lawyer can store exhibits such as documents and photographs separately or in the same folder as the first witness who will sponsor the exhibits.
For example, photographs could be filed in the witness's file or in a pocket in
the trial notebook in the subsection for that witness. A large chart would just
be brought to court. If the exhibit is a voluminous set of documents, it could
be placed in a notebook with copies for opposing counsel and the judge.

Electronically stored information can be easily accessed with a computer and displayed with a projector or on a monitor. As a backup in case there is a computer glitch, have the images printed on letter-size paper so it can be shown to the jurors. The printouts can be stored in the notebook or file folder. In a criminal case, prior to trial much of the prosecution's evidence is maintained in the evidence room of the investigating law enforcement agency.

Jury Instructions

Proposed Jury Instructions

A file folder is a suitable place for your proposed set of jury instructions until they are served and presented to the judge. You can keep a copy of yours and the other side's set of proposed instructions either in a notebook or file folder. The jury instructions chart, as well as supportive legal authority for your proposed instructions, can be kept in either a file or your trial notebook.

Pleadings

You will also have a subdivision for pleadings that can be located as with the other subdivisions either electronically, in file folders, or in notebooks. The pleadings—such as complaint, answer, amended pleadings, and so on—are also tabbed for easy retrieval.

Discovery

Discovery can be organized just as the pleadings are with subdividers in either notebooks, computer folders, or file folders. We suggest subdividers for initial disclosures, interrogatories, and responses; requests for production and responses; and requests for admissions and responses.

To-Do List

So that you do not neglect to do an essential task, have a to-do list for your case. As you complete the tasks, you can check them off. It is also important that you give due dates to the items on your list. For example: "Set deposition of "Myrna Kostich by 5/19/XX.""

Your to-do list generally will include two types of deadlines: self-imposed deadlines and those imposed by others, such as a judge's deadline for submission of a trial brief. When faced with an imposed drop-dead due date (judge-imposed deadlines are normally firm), you should schedule a due date far enough in advance of the final date so that if unforeseen events occur, as they will (your computer with no backup crashes), you can still make the deadline.

With experience, you will create a stock to-do list with time periods assigned for accomplishing each task. It is a good practice to set a finishing-touches date for the case and note it in your calendar. A finishing-touches date is set far enough out from trial that you still have time to complete any necessary task before trial. A month out from trial generally is a good length of time, but you may need to adjust the finishing-touches date for such factors as the complexity of the case. On the given finishing-touches date, review your to-do list and take stock of what needs to be done. Then, make plans with new completion dates to complete trial preparation. Ask other experienced lawyers in your jurisdiction if they have such a to-do list and whether you can adapt it to your use. This stock to-do list should be augmented for each new case.

The following is a comprehensive to-do list:

**TRIAL PREPARATION
COMPREHENSIVE TO-DO LIST**

- **Journal**—record activities
- **Thinking notes**—note ideas for opening, closing, etc.
- **Case Summary Sheet**
- Develop **case theory and themes**
  - Draft tentative closing argument
  - Conduct a case assessment
  - Draft a trial plan outline
- **Motions**
  - Prepare motions in limine to exclude and admit evidence
  - Prepare responses to motions
- **Review the files** and if needed:
  - Amend pleadings
  - Update discovery
- **Scout the court** to determine courtroom practices, preferences, and layout
- **Witnesses** for trial
  - **Subpoena** witnesses—pay statutory witness fees and costs
  - **Keep in touch** and tell them **when they will be called**
- Prepare a **trial system**—electronic case management, trial notebook, and/or file folders
- **Objections**
  - Plan to make objections and have an **objections list** for trial
  - Anticipate and plan to meet objections

- Seek and, where appropriate, enter into **stipulations and other agreements,** such as premarking exhibits with the other side
- **Court dates**
  - Check scheduled court dates
  - Set necessary hearings
  - Move to continue if needed
- **Jury selection** preparation
  - Jury consultant
  - Jury selection binder
  - Jury seating chart
  - Jury challenges chart
  - Jury selection agenda
  - Good and bad juror profiles
  - Prepare jury selection questions
  - Juror questionnaire
  - Learn about jury pool
- Prepare **opening statement**
- Prepare **direct examinations**
  - Select witnesses to call
  - Witness preparation
  - Order of witnesses
- Prepare **cross-examinations**
- Draft and organize proposed **jury instructions**
- **Exhibits and trial visuals**
  - Gather and organize real, documentary, and demonstrative evidence
  - Consultant
  - Arrange for equipment, such as document camera, monitors, LCD projector, screen, and so on
  - Exhibits list
  - Premark exhibits
  - Backup plan for computer presentation
  - Create trial visuals for all phases of trial
  - Research evidentiary foundations and prepare pocket briefs where needed
  - Arrange with the court to display visuals such as computer slideshow or to set up a document camera
- Prepare **closing argument**
- **Prepare yourself** (mentally and so on)

VI. ETHICAL CONSIDERATIONS IN CASE DEVELOPMENT AND MANAGEMENT

A. Supervising the Investigation

What are your ethical responsibilities if you are not the person conducting the interview? Instead, what are your responsibilities if your paralegal is going to conduct the witness interview?

ABA Model Rule of Professional Conduct 5.3 sets out the ethical responsibilities of a partner or managerial equivalent in a law firm or an individual lawyer directly supervising a nonlawyer employee for the conduct of that employee. Rule 5.3(a) provides that the manager is to "make reasonable efforts to ensure that the firm has in effect measures giving reasonable assurance that the person's conduct is compatible with the professional obligations of the lawyer; . . ." Under Rule 5.3(b), the direct supervising lawyer is to "make reasonable efforts to ensure that the person's conduct is compatible with the professional obligations of the lawyer; . . ."

Rule 5.3(c) states that the lawyer is responsible for any conduct of the nonlawyer that would be a violation of the rules of professional conduct if engaged in by a lawyer, if:

> (1) the lawyer orders or, with the knowledge of the specific conduct, ratifies the conduct involved; or
> (2) the lawyer is a partner or has comparable managerial authority in the law firm in which the person is employed, or has direct supervisory authority over the person, and knows of the conduct at a time when its consequences can be avoided or mitigated but fails to take reasonable remedial action.

B. The Expert

While counsel might want to find an expert who would provide testimony supporting the case theory, predisposition for favorable results is hazardous. Recall our discussion of selecting an expert in the *Bite-Mark* case, pages 36-37. The expert's bias may be apparent to the jury, or the expert may be unreliable and produce faulty results. However, when does a lawyer cross the line by employing an expert to provide favorable results and violate the rules of professional responsibility?

Clearly the line is crossed if the expert testifies falsely and the lawyer knows that the testimony is false. ABA Rule of Professional Conduct 3.3(a)(3) provides that a lawyer shall not "offer evidence that the lawyer knows to be false. If . . . a witness called by the lawyer, has offered material evidence and the lawyer comes to know of its falsity, the lawyer shall take reasonable remedial measures, including, if necessary, disclosure to the tribunal. A lawyer may refuse to offer evidence (other than the testimony of a defendant in a criminal matter) that the lawyer reasonably believes is false."

3 *The Assignments 1-84*

"With every experience, you alone are painting your own canvas, thought by thought, choice by choice."

Oprah Winfrey, *This Month's Mission*,
O The Oprah Magazine, Nov. 2001, at 290

"I hear and I forget. I see and I remember. I do and I understand."

Ancient Chinese Proverb

TABLE OF CONTENTS FOR THE ASSIGNMENTS

CHAPTERS 1 AND 2. TODAY'S TRIAL LAWYER AND TRIAL PERSUASION PRINCIPLES

CRIMINAL and CIVIL CASE ASSIGNMENTS

ASSIGNMENT 1: The Role of a Trial Attorney in the Adversary System 67

CHAPTER 3. CASE THEORY AND THEME DEVELOPMENT

CRIMINAL AND CIVIL CASE ASSIGNMENTS

ASSIGNMENT 2: Prosecutor: Case Theory and Theme Development *(Planning with the Aid of Closing Argument)* 68

ASSIGNMENT 3: Defense Attorney: Case Theory and Theme Development *(Planning with the Aid of Closing Argument)* 69

ASSIGNMENT 4:   Prosecutor and Defense Attorney: Case Fact
                 Development 71

ASSIGNMENT 5:   Prosecutor and Defense Attorney: Using Case
                 Analysis and Management Software 72

ASSIGNMENT 6:   Prosecutor and Defense Counsel: Trial
                 Preparation
                 (Witnesses, Exhibits, Trial System) 73

                 CIVIL CASE ASSIGNMENTS

ASSIGNMENT 7:   Plaintiffs' Attorney: Case Theory and Theme
                 Development
                 (Planning with the Aid of Closing Argument) 74

ASSIGNMENT 8:   Attorneys for Defendants Hard and Davola:
                 Case Theory and Theme Development
                 (Planning with the Aid of Closing Argument) 76

ASSIGNMENT 9:   Plaintiffs' and Defendants' Attorneys: Case Fact
                 Development 78

ASSIGNMENT 10:   Plaintiffs' and Defendants' Attorneys: Using Case
                 Analysis and Management Software 79

ASSIGNMENT 11:   Plaintiffs' Attorney and Attorneys for Defendants
                 Hard and Davola: Trial Preparation
                 (Witnesses, Exhibits, Trial System) 80

CHAPTER 4. TRIAL MOTION ADVOCACY

CRIMINAL CASE ASSIGNMENTS

ASSIGNMENT 12:   Prosecutor and Defense Attorney: Planning
                 Motions in Limine 81

ASSIGNMENT 13:   Prosecutor and Defense Attorney: Prosecutor's
                 Motion in Limine and Defense Response
                 (Bruno Summers's Neo-Nazi Activities) 83

ASSIGNMENT 14:   Defense Attorney and Prosecutor: Defense
                 Motion in Limine and Prosecutor Response
                 (Photographs) 85

CIVIL CASE ASSIGNMENTS

ASSIGNMENT 15:   Plaintiffs' and Defendants' Attorneys: Planning
                 Motions in Limine 86

ASSIGNMENT 16:   Attorneys for Defendant Davola and Plaintiffs:
                 Defense Motion in Limine and Plaintiffs'
                 Response
                 (Exclusion of Psychiatric Opinion) 88

CHAPTER 5. MAKING AND MEETING OBJECTIONS

CRIMINAL AND CIVIL CASE ASSIGNMENTS

ASSIGNMENT 17: Attorneys for Defendants Hard and Davola:
Making and Responding to Objections
(Peter Dean) 90

CHAPTER 6. JURY SELECTION: TWO-WAY EXCHANGE

CRIMINAL CASE ASSIGNMENTS

ASSIGNMENT 18: Prosecutor and Defense Attorney: Conducting
Jury Selection 92

CIVIL CASE ASSIGNMENTS

ASSIGNMENT 19: Plaintiffs' and Defendants' Attorneys:
Conducting Jury Selection 93

CHAPTER 7. OPENING STATEMENT: STORYTELLING

CRIMINAL AND CIVIL CASE ASSIGNMENTS

ASSIGNMENT 20: Prosecutor and Plaintiffs' Attorney: Planning
an Opening Statement 95

ASSIGNMENT 21: Defendants' Attorneys: Planning an Opening
Statement 97

ASSIGNMENT 22: Prosecutor, Plaintiffs', and Defendants' Attorneys:
Deliver an Opening Statement 98

CHAPTER 8. EXHIBITS AND THE VISUAL TRIAL

CRIMINAL AND CIVIL CASE ASSIGNMENTS

ASSIGNMENT 23: Prosecutor and Plaintiffs' Attorney: Videotape
of the Garage Tavern and Scene Visit
(Detective Tharp) 99

ASSIGNMENT 24: Prosecutor and Plaintiffs' Attorney: Scale
Diagrams of the Garage Tavern
(John Lacey, Peter Nye) 100

ASSIGNMENT 25: Prosecutor and Plaintiffs' Attorney: Photographs
of the Garage Tavern
(Detective Tharp, John Lacey, Peter Nye) 102

ASSIGNMENT 26: Prosecutor and Plaintiffs' Attorney: Skeleton
Model
(Dr. Jackson, Dr. Day) 103

ASSIGNMENT 27: Prosecutor and Plaintiffs' Attorney: Hospital
Records of Bruno Summers
(Rose Gadfly).. 104

ASSIGNMENT 28: Prosecutor and Plaintiffs' Attorney: Weapons
Applications and Check
(Fred Faye).. 105

ASSIGNMENT 29: Attorney for Defendant Hard: Scale Diagram
of the Gas Station
(John Gooding) 107

ASSIGNMENT 30: Attorney for Defendant Hard: Neo-Nazi
Membership Card
(Officer West, Rebecca Karr, Nurse Frank).................... 108

ASSIGNMENT 31: Attorneys for Defendants Hard and Davola:
Death Certificate
(Dr. Day, Dr. Jackson).............................. 109

ASSIGNMENT 32: Attorney for Defendant Hard: Bruno Summers's
Knife
(Officer West, Nurse Frank)........................... 111

ASSIGNMENT 33: Prosecutor and Plaintiffs' Attorney:
Cross-Examination with a Prior Written
Statement and Prior Conviction
(Ed Hard) 112

ASSIGNMENT 34: Attorney for Defendant Hard: Bruno Summers's
Blood Sample
(Officer Harris)...113

ASSIGNMENT 35: Attorney for Defendant Hard: Courtroom
Demonstration
(Ed Hard) 115

CRIMINAL CASE ASSIGNMENTS

ASSIGNMENT 36: Prosecutor: Gun, Rounds, and Slugs
(Officer Yale, Officer Harris, H. Tredwell) 116

CIVIL CASE ASSIGNMENTS

ASSIGNMENT 37: Plaintiffs' Attorney: Photographs
(Deborah Summers).......................................118

ASSIGNMENT 38: Plaintiffs' Attorney: Hospital, Ambulance, and
Funeral Bills
(Deborah and Hans Summers, Rose Gadfly) 120

ASSIGNMENT 39: Attorney for Defendant Hard: Medical Records
of Deborah Summers
(Dr. Sherman Croup).................................. 121

CHAPTER 9. DIRECT EXAMINATION: BUILDING THE CASE

CRIMINAL CASE ASSIGNMENTS

ASSIGNMENT 40: Defense Attorney: Preparation of Direct Examination
(John Gooding) 122

ASSIGNMENT 41: Prosecutor: Direct Examination of Fred Faye 123

ASSIGNMENT 42: Prosecutor: Direct Examination of Cindy Rigg........... 124

ASSIGNMENT 43: Prosecutor: Direct Examination of Roberta Montbank 125

ASSIGNMENT 44: Prosecutor: Direct Examination of Officer Yale *(Breathalyzer Test; Alcohol Influence Report; Opinion)* 126

ASSIGNMENT 45: Defense Attorney: Direct Examination of John Gooding *(August 26 and September 3 Incidents)* 127

CIVIL CASE ASSIGNMENTS

ASSIGNMENT 46: Plaintiffs' Attorney: Preparation of Direct Examination *(Deborah Summers)* 128

ASSIGNMENT 47: Attorney for Defendant Davola: Preparation of Direct Examination *(Tom Donaldson)* 130

ASSIGNMENT 48: Plaintiffs' Attorney: Direct Examination of Deborah Summers 131

ASSIGNMENT 49: Plaintiffs' Attorney: Direct Examination of Bert Kain 132

ASSIGNMENT 50: Plaintiffs' Attorney: Direct Examination of Roberta Montbank 133

ASSIGNMENT 51: Plaintiffs' Attorney: Direct Examination of Ronnie Summers *(Child Witness)* 134

ASSIGNMENT 52: Attorney for Defendant Hard: Direct Examination of Ed Hard 135

ASSIGNMENT 53: Attorney for Defendant Davola: Direct Examination of Mary Apple 136

CHAPTER 10. CROSS-EXAMINATION: CONCESSION SEEKING

CRIMINAL CASE ASSIGNMENTS

ASSIGNMENT 54: Defense Attorney: Cross-Examination of Peter Dean 137

ASSIGNMENT 55:   Defense Attorney: Cross-Examination of
Fred Faye 139

ASSIGNMENT 56:   Defense Attorney: Cross-Examination of
Cindy Rigg 140

ASSIGNMENT 57:   Defense Attorney: Cross-Examination of
Officer Yale 141

ASSIGNMENT 58:   Prosecutor: Cross-Examination of John Gooding 142

ASSIGNMENT 59:   Prosecutor: Cross-Examination of Ed Hard 143

CIVIL CASE ASSIGNMENTS

ASSIGNMENT 60:   Attorneys for Defendants Hard and Davola:
Cross-Examination of Deborah Summers 144

ASSIGNMENT 61:   Attorneys for Defendants Davola and Hard:
Cross-Examination of Bert Kain 145

ASSIGNMENT 62:   Attorneys for Defendants Davola and Hard:
Cross-Examination of Roberta Montbank 147

ASSIGNMENT 63:   Attorney for Defendant Hard: Cross-Examination
of Ronnie Summers 148

ASSIGNMENT 64:   Plaintiffs' Attorney: Cross-Examination of
Mary Apple 149

ASSIGNMENT 65:   Plaintiffs' Attorney: Cross-Examination of
Ed Hard 150

CHAPTER 11. EXPERTS: YOURS AND THEIRS

CRIMINAL CASE ASSIGNMENTS

ASSIGNMENT 66:   Prosecutor: Preparation of an Expert Witness
(*Dr. L.R. Jackson, Medical Examiner*) 152

ASSIGNMENT 67:   Prosecutor and Defense Attorney: Direct
Examination and Cross-Examination of an
Expert Witness
(*H. Tredwell, Firearms Expert*) 153

ASSIGNMENT 68:   Prosecutor and Defense Attorney: Direct
Examination and Cross-Examination of an
Expert Witness
(*Dr. L.R. Jackson, Medical Examiner*) 156

CIVIL CASE ASSIGNMENTS

ASSIGNMENT 69:   Plaintiffs' Attorney: Preparation of an Expert
Witness
(*Dr. Brett Day, Treating Physician*) 157

ASSIGNMENT 70: Plaintiffs' and Defendants' Attorneys: Direct
Examination and Cross-Examination of an
Expert Witness
(Dr. Brett Day, Treating Physician).............................. 159

ASSIGNMENT 71: Plaintiffs' and Defendants' Attorneys: Direct
Examination and Cross-Examination of an
Expert Witness
(Dr. Bruce Hann, Economist)...................................... 160

ASSIGNMENT 72: Defendants' and Plaintiffs' Attorneys: Direct
Examination and Cross-Examination of an
Expert Witness
(Dr. Thomas Monday, Economist)............................... 162

ASSIGNMENT 73: Attorneys for Defendant Davola and Plaintiffs:
Direct Examination and Cross-Examination
of an Expert Witness
(Dr. Dale Thompson, Hospitality Expert)...................... 164

ASSIGNMENT 74: Attorneys for Defendant Hard and Plaintiffs:
Direct Examination and Cross-Examination
of an Expert Witness
(Dr. Sherman Croup, Medical Doctor) 165

CHAPTER 12. JURY INSTRUCTIONS: THE JURY'S LAW

CRIMINAL CASE ASSIGNMENTS

ASSIGNMENT 75: Prosecutor: Preparation of Jury Instructions.............. 167
ASSIGNMENT 76: Defense Attorney: Preparation of Jury
Instructions... 168
ASSIGNMENT 77: Prosecutor and Defense Attorney: Arguing Jury
Instructions... 169

CIVIL CASE ASSIGNMENTS

ASSIGNMENT 78: Plaintiffs' Attorney: Preparation of Jury
Instructions and Verdict Forms; Arguing
Instructions... 171
ASSIGNMENT 79: Attorneys for Defendants Hard and Davola:
Preparation of Jury Instructions and Verdict
Forms; Arguing Instructions...................................... 173

CHAPTER 13. CLOSING ARGUMENT: ART OF ARGUMENT

CRIMINAL CASE ASSIGNMENTS

ASSIGNMENT 80: Prosecutor: Closing Argument.................................. 174
ASSIGNMENT 81: Defense Attorney: Closing Argument 176

CIVIL CASE ASSIGNMENTS

ASSIGNMENT 82: Plaintiffs' Attorney: Closing Argument 177

ASSIGNMENT 83: Attorney for Defendants Hard and Davola:
Closing Argument 179

THE FINAL ASSIGNMENT

ASSIGNMENT 84: Going to Trial – The Criminal or Civil Case:
State v. Hard or *Summers v. Hard* 181

ASSIGNMENTS: 1-84

Chapters 1 and 2. Today's Trial Lawyer and Trial Persuasion Principles

Criminal and Civil Case Assignments

ASSIGNMENT 1: The Role of a Trial Attorney in the Adversary System

You are about to be totally immersed in the world of a practicing trial attorney. To maximize this experience, these materials will place you in a variety of roles (plaintiff, defense, government, and private counsel) and legal arenas (civil and criminal trial preparation and trial). But always, you will be a trial advocate.

This environment, however, is more than an amalgam of skills and tactical decisions. It is a human, flesh-and-blood world in which a clear understanding of your role as a trial lawyer is a vital predicate to your effectiveness. But what is your role?

PREPARATION

READ: Chapters 1-2, *Trial Advocacy* text.

TIPS FOR ASSIGNMENT

1. What is your role and what are your responsibilities as a trial lawyer in the justice system?

    If you were sitting on a jury, what are the favorable characteristics that you would look for in a trial lawyer?

2. How do your duties differ depending on whom you represent?

3. Do you have ethical or other obligations to anyone other than your client? Be prepared to discuss questions posed.

Chapter 3. Case Theory and Theme Development

Criminal and Civil Case Assignments

ASSIGNMENT 2: Prosecutor: Case Theory and Theme Development
(Planning with the Aid of Closing Argument)

You have had a busy few weeks. Your office has charged the defendant Hard with first degree murder. At this point, it seems doubtful the case will be disposed of in any way but trial (no guilty plea, no dismissal). It is time to plan for the trial. The best way to plan for trial is to begin at the end and work backwards by having a vision of your closing argument. The outline of your argument will assist in pulling together your legal and factual theories. Moreover, it will suggest witnesses you should call, defenses you should anticipate, and demonstrative evidence to use at trial. This assignment focuses on planning your closing argument and thereby conceptualizing your case theory.

PREPARATION

READ: (1) Trial Case File Entries 1-23, 29-36, 91, 96, 97, 107; (2) Chapters 2-3, *Trial Advocacy* text.

TIPS FOR THIS ASSIGNMENT

1. The prosecutor may have the choice of arguing one or more of four legal theories: murder in the first degree, murder in the second degree, voluntary manslaughter, and involuntary manslaughter.

    If the defendant is charged with murder in the first degree, would you want the jury to be instructed on the lesser included crimes of murder in the second degree, and voluntary or involuntary manslaughter?

    Suppose that self-defense is a complete defense to all forms of homicide. Would that make any difference in whether you would want the jury to be instructed on the lesser offenses?

2. Premeditation is one of the legal elements you must prove to establish murder in the first degree. Under the pattern (standard court-approved) jury instruction on premeditation, what legal criteria must be proven to establish premeditation?

3. As you plan your argument on premeditation, consider your factual theory (story) concerning Edward Hard's premeditation in causing the death of Bruno Summers. While the prosecutor is not required to prove defendant's motive, a factual theory usually can best be understood in human terms. What would you argue to be Ed Hard's personal motivation for shooting Summers?

    When do you think Ed Hard formed the intent to cause the death of Bruno Summers?

    Suppose you conclude that Hard formed the intent to take the life of Bruno Summers on August 20, after Summers knocked him to the floor of the Garage tavern.

    Are there any weaknesses in this factual theory?

    What are the strengths of this factual theory?

4. As you contemplate how you would like to argue any of the four legal theories (murder in the first degree, etc.), what real, documentary, or demonstrative evidence or argument visual might you employ to enrich your argument?

5. A storytelling technique aids jurors in decision making. How could you use a story in presenting your case? At this point, what is your theme?

ASSIGNMENT FOR CLASS

In class, you will have a meeting of the prosecutor's office. At the meeting, you will discuss and theorize about closing argument, concentrating on developing your legal and factual case theory. At this juncture, you will not consider in depth the defense case and how you will deal with the defense theories, strengths, and vulnerabilities.

ASSIGNMENT 3: Defense Attorney: Case Theory and Theme Development
(Planning with the Aid of Closing Argument)

It appears there will be a trial. Most of your investigation and discovery and a preliminary draft of jury instructions have been completed. That makes this a good time to plan the defense case theory. Outlining the defense closing argument is an excellent way to obtain an overview of the trial to plan your strategies and to decide the jury instructions you will propose, the witnesses you will call, and the demonstrative evidence you will offer during the defense case. This assignment involves developing closing arguments on defenses and thereby conceptualizing your case theory.

PREPARATION

READ: (1) Trial Case File Entries 1-25, 29-36, 91, 96, 97, 107; (2) Chapters 2-3, *Trial Advocacy* text.

TIPS FOR THIS ASSIGNMENT

1. As defense counsel, you may argue in closing that the prosecutor has failed to meet the burden of proving the elements of the crime beyond a reasonable doubt and that you have established a defense.

   Explain what you believe is the most likely crime, and the elements of that crime, that the prosecutor might fail to prove beyond a reasonable doubt.

2. List the possible legal defenses to the charge of first degree murder. What are the defenses to murder in the second degree?

   What are the defenses to voluntary and involuntary manslaughter?

3. To prove first degree murder, the prosecutor must prove that defendant Hard premeditated, reflected more than a moment in time, and formed the intent to cause the death of Bruno Summers. Which sources of information (the prosecutor's witnesses; real, documentary, and demonstrative evidence; defense witnesses) or lack of evidence would you use to raise a reasonable doubt that Ed Hard did not premeditate?

4. Consider how you would argue self-defense.

   Suppose the court were to give the State of Major Criminal Jury Instructions on self-defense. What legal criteria must be satisfied to establish the defense of self-defense?

   What facts do you intend to elicit or prove to argue that Ed Hard acted in self-defense?

   Who will be the witnesses providing these facts?

   What weaknesses in the proof of these facts (admissibility of the evidence, witness credibility problems) do you anticipate?

   What are the strongest factual points on which you should be able to rely in arguing self-defense?

5. A storytelling technique aids jurors in the decision-making process. How would you use a story in presenting your case to a jury?

   You should present your argument concerning self-defense in human terms so it will be understood by the jury. How will you weave the facts presented in the trial case file into a human story with which the jury can empathize about Ed Hard defending himself against Bruno Summers?

   Stories help overcome a listener's bias. Is your case one in which biases should be overcome? If so, what are the biases? How will you use a story to overcome them?

   Ideas for themes are difficult to develop. At this point, what is your theme for the case?

ASSIGNMENT FOR CLASS

In class, you will hold a meeting of the defense attorney's office. At the meeting, you will discuss and theorize about your closing argument on the defenses.

ASSIGNMENT 4: Prosecutor and Defense Attorney: Case Fact Development

You have developed tentative legal and factual theories regarding the current charge of first degree murder against Edward Taylor Hard. Those theories, when placed in the context of your case strategy, will serve as guides for your investigation to find additional evidence supporting your case theory. Conversely, the results of your investigation may lead you to alter your current case theory. You have many methods available to you to obtain information. At this point, you should think broadly about their use.

For this assignment, defense counsel may assume that the *only* information you have received from the trial case files at this point is the police reports.

PREPARATION

READ: (1) Trial Case Files Entries 1-25, 29-36; (2) Trial Preparation and Case Management in this book, pages 11-57.

TIPS FOR THIS ASSIGNMENT

1. What specific information will you seek during the fact investigation? Why, in terms of your case theory, do you want it?

    What is the likely source of the information that you are seeking?

2. What precautions will you take to ensure that your investigator does not commit an ethical violation during the investigation?

ASSIGNMENT FOR CLASS

In class, discuss your case development plan from the perspective of the prosecutor and defense attorney.

ASSIGNMENT 5: Prosecutor and Defense Attorney: Using Case Analysis and Management Software

You have concluded that the *State v. Hard* case is complex enough that your organization, management, and analysis of the case may be assisted by using computer software. Your office does not own any case management software, and you would like to explore what is available and whether it would be helpful both on this case and on future cases. You have learned that companies offer potential customers an opportunity to test their software for a trial period. You decide to explore the potential use of software to assist you in the case.

For the purpose of this assignment, visit and test one or more of the Web sites referenced in Chapter 2, Trial Preparation and Case Management, in this book on pages 43-44 or a Web site selected by your instructor.

PREPARATION

READ: (1) All criminal Case Files Entries (1-36); (2) Trial Preparation and Case Management in this book on pages 11-57; and (3) Internet exploration of Web sites offering software for case management and analysis.

TIPS FOR THIS ASSIGNMENT

1. What does the software that you tested offer in terms of case organization, management, and analysis?

2. Describe your experiences using the Web sites.

3. Are there any concerns that you have about your firm purchasing the software (such as expense, time devoted to entering the case data, other)?

ASSIGNMENT FOR CLASS

In class, discuss your experience with the software, the feasibility of purchasing the software, and what it can do for your case and future cases handled by your office.

ASSIGNMENT 6: Prosecutor and Defense Counsel: Trial Preparation (*Witnesses, Exhibits, Trial System*)

Preparing to present your case is somewhat, although not entirely, analogous to the process that a chef goes through in deciding the menu for a formal dinner—selecting the recipes, the ingredients, and the order of the items to be served during the dinner.

With this analogy partly in mind, you now need to design how you will present your case in order to most effectively communicate your case theory to the jury. During this phase of trial preparation, you ponder which witnesses you will call in your case-in-chief, the order of witnesses, the exhibits you wish to have admitted into evidence, the organization of the trial material in a trial system, and a general list of things to do.

PREPARATION

READ: (1) Trial Case File Entries 1-36, 91, 96, 97; (2) Trial Preparation and Case Management in this book, pages 11-57.

TIPS FOR THIS ASSIGNMENT

1. You must develop an order for presenting your witnesses. The conventional wisdom for originating the order of witnesses is to start strong, finish strong, and bury any weaknesses in the middle. Of your witnesses, which one would you select to lead off your case-in-chief?

   Which one would you select to be your final witness? Which witnesses are you compelled to call but most likely would insert in the middle of the presentation of your case-in-chief? Explain.

2. You need not call every witness who may have some information to present to the jury. Some evidence presented would be merely cumulative. Some evidence is of little consequence to the real issues in the lawsuit. Consider which witnesses you will not call to testify. However, you as prosecutor must always remember that the defense may use in argument your failure to call a witness. For instance, the defense may refer to the fact that a particular witness was not called and then use this fact, arguing that a reasonable doubt may be derived not only from the evidence but from the lack of evidence.

    Of all the witnesses available, compose a list of those witnesses whom you do not intend to call.

3. Trial lawyers need a trial system to organize and retrieve trial materials. They may be filed in a trial notebook, files, or a computer. Think about the content and organization that will be most helpful to you in a trial notebook. What trial system will you use?

    How will you organize the information?

4. As the trial date grows closer, you will have many things that will need to be prepared. What will be on your to-do list to prepare for trial (prepare general and specific questions for voir dire)?

    Construct a schedule for focusing on these tasks.

ASSIGNMENT FOR CLASS

In class, be prepared to discuss the order of witnesses, your strategy for placing them in that order, the exhibit list, and how you intend to call the listed witnesses to establish foundations for the admissibility of the exhibits. Be prepared to discuss your organizational system for trial.

Civil Case Assignments

ASSIGNMENT 7: Plaintiffs' Attorney: Case Theory and Theme Development
(Planning with the Aid of Closing Argument)

You have had a busy few weeks. Most of discovery has been completed, and it is doubtful the case against the defendants—Edward Hard, M.C. Davola, and Davola's employees, Mary Apple and Tom Donaldson—will be resolved out of court. It is time to begin planning for the trial. The best way to plan for trial is to begin at the end and work backwards by having a vision of your closing argument. The outline of your argument will pull together your legal and factual theories. Moreover, it will suggest witnesses you should call, defenses you should anticipate, and demonstrative evidence to use at trial. This assignment focuses on planning your closing argument and thereby conceptualizing your case theory.

PREPARATION

READ: (1) Trial Case File Entries 1-88, 92, 96, 98, 118; (2) Chapters 2-3, *Trial Advocacy* text.

TIPS FOR THIS ASSIGNMENT

1. As plaintiffs' attorney, you have the burden of proving the elements of your claims for relief in order to obtain a remedy for wrongful death. This is a principal part of your legal theory. During closing argument, you will argue that when the law (elements of the claim) is applied to the facts, plaintiffs have proved their claims by a preponderance of the evidence.

   What elements must be proven to establish negligence by defendant Hard? Davola?

   What elements must be proven to establish negligence per se by Hard? Davola?

   What elements must be proven for Deborah Summers to establish emotional distress?

   What elements must be proven for Ronnie Summers to establish emotional distress?

2. In every wrongful death trial, plaintiffs must prove damages as an element. What are the elements of damages for Bruno Summers's wrongful death? What sources of information (witnesses, exhibits) would you like to argue to prove damages? What weaknesses, if any, do you foresee in the proof of facts on damages?

   What argument would you present on the issue of damages?

3. You will best be able to anticipate what most likely will occur at trial and identify defenses you will need to meet by stepping into the shoes of defense counsel and examining the trial from a defense perspective. If you were defense counsel, what are all the possible defenses you might raise on behalf of defendant Ed Hard? Davola? Apple? Donaldson?

Of those defenses, which are the strongest defenses you would choose if you were defense counsel? Why?

ASSIGNMENT FOR CLASS

You will have a meeting of the plaintiffs' attorney in class. At the meeting, you will discuss and theorize about your closing argument, concentrating on developing your legal and factual case theories. Also, consider in depth the defense case and how you will deal with defense theories, strengths, and vulnerabilities.

ASSIGNMENT 8: Attorneys for Defendants Hard and Davola: Case Theory and Theme Development *(Planning with the Aid of Closing Argument)*

It appears there will be a trial. Most of the discovery has been completed. That makes this a good time to plan the defense case theory. Outlining the defense closing argument is an excellent way to obtain an overview of the trial. Using your outline of closing argument, you can plan your strategies and decide the jury instructions you will propose and rely on, determine the witnesses you will present; and plan the demonstrative evidence you will offer. This problem involves developing closing arguments for the defense and thereby conceptualizing your case theory.

PREPARATION

READ: (1) Trial Case File Entries 1-88, 96, 98, 100, 118; (2) Chapters 2-3.

TIPS FOR THIS ASSIGNMENT

Think about the following three sets of questions by assuming the role either of attorney for defendant Hard or attorney for defendant Davola.

1. As defense counsel, you may argue in closing that the plaintiffs have failed to meet the burden of proving the elements of their claims by a preponderance of evidence and that you have established a defense. Analyze the trial case file and jury instructions.

   Explain what you believe are the most likely claims that plaintiffs might fail to prove by a preponderance of the evidence.

List all the potential legal defenses to the wrongful death claim based on a legal theory of negligence.

What are the defenses to negligence per se?

What are the defenses to intentional tort of battery?

2. Based on your review of the case at this point, you believe plaintiffs will most likely try to prove common law negligence. To prove common law negligence, plaintiffs must prove that defendant Hard acted unreasonably and carelessly in causing the death of Bruno Summers.

   Which facts would you wish to argue in support of the defense that defendant did not act unreasonably or carelessly to cause the killing?

   What sources of information (the plaintiffs' witnesses; real, documentary, and demonstrative evidence; defense witnesses) or lack of evidence would you use to argue that Ed Hard did not act unreasonably or carelessly?

3. Failure of plaintiffs to prove negligence and the defense of self-defense are merely two of the possible defenses available to defendant Hard. You need to consider how you would argue every defense, for example, unavoidable accident, contributory negligence, or vilification of Bruno Summers's character (not technically a defense, but a strategy that could make the jury apathetic about finding liability). For each plausible defense, think about what sources of information (plaintiffs' witnesses, defense witnesses, exhibits) you would like to argue in support of the defense.

   What weaknesses do you detect in the defense? Is the defense so vulnerable to attack that to present this defense theory would undermine the credibility of other defense theories?

   Is the defense intrinsically inconsistent with another defense?

   How would you argue that the law on the defense applies to the facts of the case?

Now consider the potential defenses the defendants (Davola, Apple, Donaldson, and Hard) might present as you take into account the next two sets of questions.

4. The defenses that each defendant could potentially present may be legally consistent but factually harmful to another defendant. For example, if Ed Hard alleges contributory negligence by Bruno

Summers and argues that it was "a well-known fact that Bruno Summers was a violent man," Davola's factual theory that he and his employees could not foresee violence might be weakened. Analyze each potential defense and determine which are factually consistent for all defendants.

Which defenses are the strongest for each of the defendants?

Which defenses are the weakest for each of the defendants?

Is there any way that the factual theories for the potentially strong defenses can be argued consistently?

5. A storytelling technique aids jurors in the decision-making process. How would you use a story in presenting your case to a jury? Stories help overcome a listeners' bias. Is your case one in which biases should be overcome? If so, what are the biases?

How will you use a story to overcome them?

Ideas for themes are difficult to develop. At this juncture, what is your case theme?

ASSIGNMENT FOR CLASS

In class, you will hold a meeting for defense attorneys. At the meeting, you will discuss and theorize about your closing argument for the defenses.

ASSIGNMENT 9: Plaintiffs' and Defendants' Attorneys: Case Fact Development

You have developed tentative legal and factual theories regarding *Summers v. Hard*. Those theories, when placed in the context of your tentative representational strategies, will serve as guides for your factual investigation. Conversely, the results of your factual investigation may lead you to alter your current case theory. You have many methods available to you to obtain information. At this point, you should think broadly about their use.

PREPARATION

READ: (1) Trial Case Files Entries 1-36, 47, 68-88, 92, 96, 98; and (2) Trial Preparation and Case Management in this book, pages 11-57.

TIPS FOR THIS ASSIGNMENT

1. What specific information will you seek during the fact investigation? Why, in terms of your case theory, do you want it?

   What is the likely source of the information that you are seeking?

2. What precautions will you take to ensure that your investigator does not commit an ethical violation during the investigation?

ASSIGNMENT FOR CLASS

In class, discuss your case development plan from the perspective of both plaintiffs and defendants.

ASSIGNMENT 10: Plaintiffs' and Defendants' Attorneys: Using Case Analysis and Management Software

You have concluded that the *Summers v. Hard* case is complex enough that your trial organization, management, and analysis of the case may be assisted by using computer software. Your law office does not own any case management software. You would like to explore what is available and whether it would be helpful both on this case and on future cases. You have learned that companies offer potential customers an opportunity to test their software for trial periods. You decide to explore the potential use of software to assist you in the case.

For the purpose of this assignment, visit and test one or more of the Web sites referenced in Chapter 2 in this book, pages 43-44 or a Web site selected by your instructor.

PREPARATION

READ: (1) All Trial Case Files Entries (1-88); (2) Internet exploration of Web sites offering software for case management and analysis; and (3) Trial Preparation and Case Management in this book, pages 11-57.

TIPS FOR THIS ASSIGNMENT

1. What does the software that you tested offer in terms of case organization, management and analysis? Describe your experiences using the Web sites.

2. Are there concerns that you have about your firm purchasing the software such as expense, time devoted to entering the case data, other?

ASSIGNMENT FOR CLASS

In class, discuss your experience with the software, the feasibility of purchasing the software, and what it can do for your case and future cases handled by your office.

ASSIGNMENT 11: Plaintiffs' Attorney and Attorneys for Defendants Hard and Davola: Trial Preparation (*Witnesses, Exhibits, Trial System*)

Preparing to present your case is somewhat, although not entirely, analogous to the process that a chef goes through in deciding the menu for a formal dinner—selecting the recipes, the ingredients, and the order of the items to be served during the dinner.

With this analogy partly in mind, you now need to design how you will present your case in order to most effectively communicate your case theory to the jury. During this phase of trial preparation, you ponder which witnesses you will call in your case-in-chief, the order of witnesses, the exhibits you wish to have admitted into evidence, the organization of the trial material in a trial system, and a general list of things to do.

PREPARATION

READ: (1) Trial Case File Entries 1-36, 92, 96, 98; and (2) Trial Preparation and Case Management in this book, pages 11-57.

TIPS FOR THIS ASSIGNMENT

1. You must develop an order for presenting your witnesses. The conventional wisdom for originating the order of witnesses is to start strong, finish strong, and bury any weaknesses in the middle. Of your witnesses, which one would you select to lead off your case-in-chief?

    Which one would you select to be your final witness?

    Which witnesses are you compelled to call but most likely would insert in the middle of the presentation of your case-in-chief?

2. You need not call every witness who may have some information to present to the jury. Some evidence presented would be merely cumulative. Some evidence is of little consequence to the real issues in the lawsuit. Consider which witnesses you will not call to testify. However, you as plaintiff must always remember that the defense may use in argument your failure to call a witness. For instance, the defense may refer to the fact that a particular witness was not called and then use this fact, arguing that weakness in your claims may be derived not only from the evidence but also from the lack of evidence. Of all the witnesses available, compose a list of those witnesses whom you do not intend to call.

3. Trial lawyers need a trial system to organize and retrieve trial materials. They may be filed in a trial notebook, files, or a computer. What trial system will you use?

   How will you organize the information?

4. As the trial date grows closer, you will have many things that will need to be prepared. What will be on your to-do list to prepare for trial (prepare general and specific questions for voir dire)?

   Construct a schedule for focusing on these tasks.

ASSIGNMENT FOR CLASS

In class, be prepared to discuss the order of witnesses, your strategy for placing them in that order, the exhibit list, and how you intend to call the listed witnesses to establish foundations for the admissibility of the exhibits. Be prepared to discuss your organizational system for trial.

Chapter 4. Trial Motion Advocacy

Criminal Case Assignments

ASSIGNMENT 12: Prosecutor and Defense Attorney: Planning Motions in Limine

It is a few weeks before trial; it is time to plan and prepare the motions in limine each side will present to the trial judge prior to the commencement of the trial.

Preparing for and defending a motion in limine requires that an attorney think in three steps and then integrate these steps. The first step is to think about the significance of the subject or point to be presented in a motion in limine. The second step is to examine the motion legal theory that supports the position to be taken in the motion. The third step is to do the factual planning and assemble the factual evidence that will be presented to support or oppose the motion. In all three steps, both prosecutor and defense counsel should consider their positions and their opponents' positions and then plan related strategies.

PREPARATION

READ: (1) Trial Case File Entries 1-36, 91, 94, 95, 100, 101, 111; (2) Chapter 4, *Trial Advocacy* text.

TIPS FOR THIS ASSIGNMENT

In preparing and arguing motions, you should think about your own and your adversary's positions by first assuming the role of the prosecutor and then the role of the defense counsel.

1. Initially, you will want to think in broad terms about the witness testimony and exhibits and trial visuals that the opposing party may offer at trial and then identify which evidence you would like to exclude through a motion in limine.

   List all seriously harmful evidence the opposing party may attempt to present during the trial.

   Next, review your list and specify the evidence you tentatively will attempt to exclude through a motion in limine.

   What items on the list will you object to during the trial?

   What criteria did you use for selecting the items to exclude by motion in limine rather than by a trial objection?

2. Motions in limine also can be made to prohibit opposing counsel from making certain statements in the presence of the jury.

   List the motions in limine that you would make in this regard.

   What anticipated statements of opposing counsel would you object to at trial?

3. You know the defense has employed a polygrapher, Jim Raven.

   Would you make a motion in limine to exclude any reference to the polygraph examination?

What response might the defense make to your motion?

If it were the established law in the State of Major that polygraph examinations are inadmissible, why not reserve your objection until it appears there may be a mention of the polygraph during the trial?

If defense counsel were to mention the polygraph during trial, what remedies do you have to cure the problem?

ASSIGNMENT FOR CLASS

In class, be prepared to discuss in limine motions. Assume the role of the prosecutor and then the role of the defense counsel, unless your instructor indicates otherwise.

ASSIGNMENT 13: Prosecutor and Defense Attorney: Prosecutor's Motion in Limine and Defense Response (*Bruno Summers's Neo-Nazi Activities*)

It is now a few weeks before trial. The prosecution has reason to believe that defendant Hard will attempt to present evidence that the victim, Bruno Summers, was a member of a neo-Nazi survivalist group. Not surprisingly, the prosecution would like to present a motion in limine to exclude from evidence any mention of Bruno Summers being a neo-Nazi or belonging to a survivalist group or his activities with the group. On the other hand, defense counsel will oppose any motion to exclude evidence of Bruno Summers's neo-Nazi activities.

PREPARATION

READ: (1) Trial Case File Entries 1-36, 91, 94, 95 (Rules 401-404), 100; (2) Chapter 4, *Trial Advocacy* text.

TIPS FOR THIS ASSIGNMENT

In preparing and arguing motions, you should think through both your own and your adversary's positions. First assume the role of the prosecutor and then the role of the defense counsel.

1. Commence your motion planning by thinking about the significance of this motion. How does defendant Hard's theory of the case benefit

if he is able to present evidence of Bruno Summers's neo-Nazi status and activities?

How significant is evidence of Bruno Summers's neo-Nazi status likely to be to a jury?

2. The second step is to plan your motion legal theory. What is the defense's motion legal theory for admission of Bruno Summers's neo-Nazism?

    Are there problems with the defense's motion legal theory? If so, explain how the prosecutor could take advantage of such problems.

3. What is the prosecution's motion legal theory for excluding evidence of Summers's neo-Nazism? What will be defendant Hard's reply?

    What reasons could the prosecutor have to forgo making this motion in limine?

    What concerns is a judge likely to have when considering admission of Bruno Summers's neo-Nazi status and activities into evidence?

4. Consider discussing Bruno Summers's neo-Nazi activities during your opening statement in spite of the fact that the judge has ruled in limine that the evidence is inadmissible. Remember the following: You believe the court's decision is wrong; you have a duty to fully represent your client; the state cannot appeal; the court probably will not grant a mistrial and, rather, will at most instruct the jury to disregard your statement. Why not do it?

ASSIGNMENT IN CLASS

Assume the role of the prosecutor and then the role of the defense counsel, unless your instructor indicates otherwise. Your instructor will inform you which part of the assignment to prepare.

1. Outside of class: (a) Prosecutor, write a motion in limine and a memorandum in support of the motion to exclude Bruno Summers's neo-Nazism. (b) Defense attorney, write a response to the prosecutor's motion.

2. In class: Attorneys for both parties argue the motion in limine.

ASSIGNMENT 14: Defense Attorney and Prosecutor: Defense Motion in Limine and Prosecutor Response *(Photographs)*

It is a few weeks before the trial is set to begin. The defense attorney believes that the prosecutor will in all likelihood try to offer into evidence two sets of photographs: (1) the photographs of Bruno Summers that were taken by a Garage tavern right after Bruno Summers was shot and (2) the photographs of Bruno Summers with his family. The defense would like to exclude or prevent any mention of these photographs during the course of the trial.

PREPARATION

READ: (1) Trial Case File Entries 1-36, 91, 94, 95 (Rules 401-403, 901), 111, 122; (2) Chapter 4, *Trial Advocacy* text.

TIPS FOR THIS ASSIGNMENT

In preparing and arguing motions, you should think through both your own and your adversary's positions by first assuming the role of defense counsel and then the role of the prosecutor.

1. Begin your analysis by thinking about the motion. How does the prosecution's theory of the case benefit if it is able to present (1) the Garage tavern photographs and (2) the family photographs? What is the probative value of each photograph?

   If the court allows the photographs to be introduced as evidence, what approaches would you take as defense attorney to reduce the impact of each of the photographs?

2. Now plan your motion legal theory. What is the prosecution's motion legal theory for admission of the Garage tavern photographs? The family photographs?

   What will defendant Hard's attorney affirmatively argue?

3. Next, do your factual planning and assemble the evidence supporting your motion. As the prosecutor, what factual record, if any, should be presented for a foundation for each of these photographs?

   As defense counsel, what legal arguments would you present concerning the exclusion of the Garage tavern photographs? The family photographs?

4. Finally, prosecutor, think ahead and consider your trial strategy on the assumption that the trial judge granted the defense motion in limine to exclude the photographs. Would you ask Detective Tharp on direct examination whether the Garage tavern photographs would aid him in explaining his testimony, knowing that he would give a positive response?

Is there any ethical problem with this question?

ASSIGNMENT FOR CLASS

Assume the role of the prosecutor and then the role of the defense counsel, unless your instructor indicates otherwise. Your instructor will inform you which part of the assignment to prepare.

1. Outside of class: (a) Defense attorney, write a motion in limine and a memorandum in support of your motion to exclude the Garage tavern photographs and the family photographs.

    (b) Prosecutor, write a memorandum in response to the defense motion.

2. In class: Attorneys for the parties, prepare to argue the motion.

Civil Case Assignments

ASSIGNMENT 15: Plaintiffs' and Defendants' Attorneys: Planning Motions in Limine

It is a few weeks before trial; it is time to plan and prepare the in limine motions each side will present to the trial judge prior to the commencement of the trial.

Preparing for and defending a motion in limine requires that an attorney think in three steps and then integrate these steps. The first step is to think about the significance of the subject or point to be presented in a motion in limine. The second step is to examine the motion legal theory that supports the position to be taken in the motion. The third step is to do the factual planning and assemble the factual evidence that will be presented to support or oppose the motion. In all three steps, both plaintiffs' and defendants' counsel should consider their positions and their opponents' positions and then plan related strategies.

PREPARATION

READ: (1) Trial Case File Entries 1-88, 92-96, 98, 100, 101, 111, 118, 122; (2) Chapter 4, *Trial Advocacy* text.

TIPS FOR THIS ASSIGNMENT

In preparing and arguing motions, you should think through both your own and your adversary's positions. When there are multiple defendants, consider each defendant's position by first assuming the role of plaintiffs' attorney and then the role of the defense counsel.

1.   Plaintiffs' attorney, imagine that defense counsel intends to inquire on Deborah Summers's cross-examination about her sexual relations with Ed Hard. As plaintiffs' attorney, would you make a motion in limine to prohibit defense counsel from referring to this subject?

     What would be your motion legal authority and argument? How do you think the defense will respond?

2.   Defense counsel, consider some specific information that you may attempt to exclude through a motion in limine. Would you make a motion to exclude any reference to the alleged August 22 telephone call by Edward Hard to Deborah and Bruno Summers?

     Suppose you decided to make the motion. What would be your legal authority and argument?

     How do you expect plaintiffs' attorney to respond to your motion?

3.   Defendant Hard's attorney, suppose that at a pretrial hearing before a motions judge (a different judge from the trial judge) your motion in limine to exclude photographs taken at the Garage tavern after the shooting was denied without prejudice as premature. Would you renew your motion to the trial judge before the jury was selected?

     Would you renew your motion when plaintiffs call Dr. Risseen, the medical doctor who treated Deborah Summers?

     When plaintiffs try to enter the photos through the doctor?

ASSIGNMENT FOR CLASS

When there are multiple defendants, consider each defendant's position by first assuming the role of the plaintiffs' attorney and then the role of the defense attorney. In class, be prepared to discuss in limine motions.

ASSIGNMENT 16: Attorneys for Defendant Davola and Plaintiffs: Defense Motion in Limine and Plaintiffs' Response
(Exclusion of Psychiatric Opinion)

Plaintiffs' attorney hired an expert witness, Dr. David Bowman, a clinical psychologist. Defendant Davola's attorney learned at Dr. Bowman's deposition that Dr. Bowman is prepared to give an opinion that a layperson, and, in particular, Tom Donaldson and Mary Apple, could have predicted that violence would occur between Bruno Summers and Edward Hard. Defendant Davola has also hired an expert, Dr. Hollis Lufkin, who will testify that no one can predict behavior accurately.

Not surprisingly, defendant Davola's attorney would like to present a motion in limine to exclude all psychiatric and psychological expert witness testimony. Defendant Hard has not yet taken a position on this motion.

Preparing for and defending a motion in limine requires that an attorney think in three steps and then integrate these steps. The first step is to think about the significance of the subject or point to be presented in a motion in limine. The second step is to examine the motion legal theory that supports the position to be taken in the motion. The third step is to do the factual planning and assemble the factual evidence that will be presented to support or oppose the motion. In all three steps, both plaintiffs' and defendant Davola's attorney should consider their positions and their opponents' positions and then plan related strategies.

PREPARATION

READ: (1) Trial Case File Entries 1-88, 92, 94, 95 (Rules 401-403, 702, 703), 98, 110, 113, 118, 121; (2) Chapter 4, *Trial Advocacy* text.

TIPS FOR THIS ASSIGNMENT

In preparing and arguing motions, you should think through both your own and opposing counsel's positions by first assuming the role of defendant Davola's attorney and then the role of plaintiffs' attorney.

1. Defendant Davola's attorney, commence your general planning of your motion by analyzing the significance of the testimony you wish to exclude.

How does plaintiffs' theory of the case benefit if plaintiffs present Dr. Bowman's expert testimony? How significant is Dr. Bowman's expert opinion likely to be to a jury?

2. Both attorneys must now plan their legal theories.

    What is the plaintiffs' motion legal theory for admission of Dr. Bowman's testimony?

    What is defendant Davola's motion legal theory for excluding Dr. Bowman's testimony?

    What will defendant Davola affirmatively argue?

3. Now you need to gather the evidence in support of the motion and do factual planning. As plaintiffs' attorney, what factual record or offer of proof, if any, should be presented as a foundation for admission of the expert opinion testimony?

    What will be the specific source of plaintiffs' attorney's factual record (witnesses, documents)?

4. As defendant Davola's attorney, what general line of defense would you present concerning the reliability of Dr. Bowman's expert testimony?

    If you would present witnesses, what type of witnesses would you call?

    Would you present your expert witness, Dr. Lufkin?

ASSIGNMENT FOR CLASS

In preparing and arguing motions, first assume the role of defendant Davola's attorney and then the role of plaintiffs' attorney, unless your instructor indicates otherwise. Your instructor will inform you which part of the assignment to prepare.

1. Outside of class: (a) Attorney for defendant Davola, write a motion in limine to exclude Dr. Bowman's testimony and opinion. (b) Plaintiffs' attorney, prepare written opposition to the motion.

2. In class: Attorneys for Davola and plaintiffs, prepare to argue the motion.

Chapter 5. Making and Meeting Objections

Criminal and Civil Case Assignments

ASSIGNMENT 17: Attorneys for Defendants Hard and Davola: Making and Responding to Objections (Peter Dean)

Assume that the prosecutor or plaintiffs' attorney will call Peter Dean to testify. Peter Dean is 31 years old and unmarried. He graduated from Roosevelt High School one year before Bruno Summers; they were best friends during their school years. Dean attended Green Lake Community College for two years and graduated. He then attended Ruston University part-time at night, graduating after six years with a liberal arts degree. While attending college, Dean worked part-time as a truck driver for United Food, a food distribution trucking firm. After graduating from college, he had difficulty finding employment. He eventually was hired by Sunflower Dairy as a delivery person of milk and other dairy products. He has been employed by the dairy for six years.

Peter Dean will testify: He was a friend of Bruno and Deborah Summers, he was at the home of Bruno's parents on August 22 when Ed Hard allegedly made a threatening telephone call to Bruno, and he witnessed some events at the Garage tavern on September 3.

PREPARATION

READ: (1) Trial Case File Entries 1-36, 72, 95 (Rules 104, 401-404, 801, 803, 901); (2) Chapter 5, *Trial Advocacy* text.

TIPS FOR THIS ASSIGNMENT

For the purposes of learning and practicing how to make and respond to objections, it is important that you anticipate the objections that can be made on direct examination and plan to object. For this assignment, focus on the prosecutor or plaintiffs' witness Peter Dean and plan to make objections during his direct examination and cross-examination testimony.

1. Plan for when you will object. Generally, you will want to object only when the evidence or the actions of opposing counsel harm your

case. From your review of Peter Dean's biography and prior state-ment, what evidence is objectionable and hurts your case?

If counsel attempts to elicit the evidence you have listed as objection-able and harmful, how will you phrase your objection?

What arguments, legal and factual, will you make in support of your objection?

2. In order to respond to objections that might be made to your cross-examination, you need to plan cross-examination of Peter Dean. Then you can analyze the cross-examination to determine when it is likely the prosecutor or plaintiffs' attorney will object.

    Outline your cross-examination of Peter Dean, listing the major points you wish to cover. Consider each point and exhibit in your outline. What potential objections might be made?

    What legal argument could the prosecutor or plaintiffs' attorney make as to each point or exhibit?

    What factual argument could the prosecutor or plaintiffs' attorney potentially make in support of the objection? How would you respond to each objection?

3. Specifically, imagine that you wish to ask on cross-examination whether Peter Dean is or was a member in Bruno Summers's neo-Nazi organization. What objections may the prosecutor or plaintiffs' attorney make to such an examination?

    What legal and factual arguments could you make to respond to the objection?

ASSIGNMENT FOR CLASS

Your instructor will tell you to assume the role of either attorney for defen-dant Hard or defendant Davola in *State v. Hard*, or attorney for defendant Hard in *Summers v. Hard*. In class, the direct and cross-examination of Peter Dean will be conducted. (Your instructor may decide to use a transcript of Peter Dean's testimony because you have not studied those topics yet.) Be prepared to object as the prosecutor or as plaintiffs' attorney presents the direct testimony of Peter Dean. You should make every possible objection because this exercise is designed to develop and refine your skills in making objections and arguing in support of them.

Be prepared to respond to the prosecutor's or plaintiffs' attorney's objec-tions during cross-examination.

Chapter 6. Jury Selection: Two-Way Exchange

Criminal Case Assignments

ASSIGNMENT 18: Prosecutor and Defense Attorney: Conducting Jury Selection

You have already thought about the end of the trial by analyzing your case and preparing a tentative closing argument. Now it is time to think about the beginning of the trial—jury selection. In Judge Watson's court, after the judge and attorneys have asked general questions of all prospective jurors, you and opposing counsel will have opportunities to question prospective jurors.

PREPARATION

READ: (1) Trial Case File Entries 1-36, 91, 94-96, 97, 106; (2) Chapter 6, *Trial Advocacy* text.

TIPS FOR THIS ASSIGNMENT

1. This assignment addresses two steps in your preparation for jury selection. The first is to prepare the questions that you may want to ask the prospective jurors. The second is to prepare for contingencies during voir dire. Planning for contingencies includes thinking about objections your opponent may make to your voir dire questions, your follow-up questions based on responses of prospective jurors to your initial questions, peremptory challenges, challenges for cause, and rehabilitation of jurors challenged for cause.

   State your specific objectives for jury selection in *State v. Hard.*

2. You want to get a sense of the individual jurors during your questioning; therefore, you want to ask open-ended questions ("Could you tell us what your duties are in your job as . . . ?") that will allow the jurors to talk.

   What open-ended questions would you ask to elicit a free flow of information from the jurors?

3. Prosecutor, imagine it is clear that a prospective juror was a close personal friend of Bruno Summers, the defense has challenged the juror for cause, and the law does not require the court to excuse the juror.

Give reasons why you would agree to the juror being excused. Give reasons why you would argue that the juror should not be excused.

Which do you believe is the better response?

4. Prosecutor, envision a situation where you exercise a peremptory challenge that would excuse a person of Jewish ancestry from the jury panel. What action, if any, might the defense take?

Suppose that during the entire jury selection you exercise three peremptories to excuse all persons of Jewish ancestry from the panel.

What action might the defense take?

Assume that the defense moves to have the court compel you to state on the record why you are excusing these jurors. Would you automatically explain the basis for your peremptory challenge?

What factual argument would you make in response to this motion?

Legal argument?

Would the same issues be raised if, instead of a criminal case, this was a civil case for wrongful death of Bruno Summers?

ASSIGNMENT FOR CLASS

For this assignment, assume the role either of prosecutor or defense attorney unless your instructor indicates a specific role. (1) Be prepared to discuss jury selection, the types of jurors that you would like to include and exclude from your jury, and jury selection strategies and challenges. (2) Be prepared to engage in voir dire.

Civil Case Assignments

ASSIGNMENT 19: Plaintiffs' and Defendants' Attorneys: *Conducting Jury Selection*

You have already thought about the end of the trial by analyzing your case and preparing a tentative closing argument. Now it is time to think about the beginning of the trial—jury selection. In Judge Mamone's court, after the judge and attorneys have asked several questions of all prospective jurors, you and opposing counsel will have opportunities to question each individual prospective juror.

PREPARATION

READ: (1) Trial Case File Entries 1-88, 92-96, 98, 106, 118; (2) Chapter 6, *Trial Advocacy* text.

TIPS FOR THIS ASSIGNMENT

1. There are two steps to your preparation for jury selection. The first is to prepare the questions that you may want to ask the prospective jurors. The second is to prepare for contingencies during voir dire. Planning for contingencies includes thinking about objections your opponent may make to your voir dire questions, your follow-up questions based on responses of prospective jurors to your initial questions, peremptory challenges, challenges for cause, and rehabilitation of jurors challenged for cause. State your specific objectives for voir dire in *Summers v. Hard.*

2. You want to get the sense of the individual jurors during your questioning; therefore, you want to ask open-ended questions that will allow the jurors to talk. What initial questions would you ask to elicit a free flow of information from the jurors?

3. You want to make sure that the individual jurors will give a fair hearing both to your legal and factual theories of the case.

    What specific questions concerning your case theory do you plan to ask?

    What specific questions concerning your case theory, permissible under the court's normal guidelines, could you ask on the following subjects:

    (1) Negligence?

    (2) Self-defense?

    (3) Foreseeability?

    (4) Contributory negligence?

    (5) Preponderance of the evidence?

4. Plaintiffs' attorney, think about how you might use the jury selection process to candidly disclose weaknesses in your case. Imagine that you believe Bruno Summers's neo-Nazi activities will be admissible during the trial. You wish to confront the jury with this fact and condition them to receive it without undue prejudice.

What artfully drawn questions might you ask to accomplish this result?

5. Defense counsel, what are the weaknesses in your case?

   What artfully drawn questions might you ask to condition the jury to receive information on the weaknesses without undue prejudice?

6. Defense counsel, a friend of yours—a professor of psychology—has advised you that persons of German ancestry are more likely to favor plaintiffs' case. Suppose that the defense exercises a peremptory challenge excusing a person of German ancestry from the jury panel. What action, if any, might the plaintiffs' attorney take?

   Suppose that the defense uses three peremptory challenges to excuse persons of German ancestry. Assume that plaintiffs' attorney moves to have the court compel you to state on the record why you are excusing jurors of German ancestry.

   Would you automatically explain the basis for your peremptory challenges?

   What factual argument would you make in response to this motion? Legal argument?

ASSIGNMENT FOR CLASS

For this assignment, assume the role of either plaintiffs' or defense attorney, unless your instructor indicates a specific role. (1) Be prepared to discuss your jury selection questions, the types of jurors that you would like to include and exclude from your jury, jury selection strategies, and challenges. (2) Be prepared to engage in jury selection.

Chapter 7. Opening Statement: Storytelling

Criminal and Civil Case Assignments

ASSIGNMENT 20: Prosecutor and Plaintiffs' Attorney: Planning an Opening Statement

You are preparing for trial, and it is time to think about and plan your opening statement. You are aware of the importance of your opening statement; you have the opportunity to make the first opening statement and a favorable impression on the jury. An effective opening will be the result of your trial preparation and planning.

PREPARATION

READ: (1) Trial Case File Entries 1-36, 92, 94-96, 109 (criminal case); (2) Trial Case File Entries 1-88, 92-96, 98, 109, 118 (civil case); (3) Chapter 7, *Trial Advocacy* text.

TIPS FOR THIS ASSIGNMENT

1. An effective opening statement communicates the attorney's case theory clearly. What is your theory of the case?

   What is your case theme? What key factual points do you wish to stress?

   The words you select to convey those factual points are important. What powerful words would you select to emphasize your key points, without being argumentative?

2. The structure you use for the organization of your opening statement will determine whether the thoughts you wish to communicate are readily understood by the jury.

   Will you use a narrative approach?

   A flashback approach?

   Any other structure in this case?

3. You wish to seize the jurors' attention with the introductory remarks of your opening statement. How might you begin your opening?

4. It is a well-established principle that if there is a significant weakness in your case, you should eliminate the sting during opening statement by confessing the weakness and attempting to defuse it.

   List the weak points in your case.

   How will you attempt to defuse those weak points in your opening statement?

5. As you think about ways to communicate with the jury, consider using visuals during your opening statement. What visuals might assist you in communicating information to the jury?

ASSIGNMENT FOR CLASS

Assume the role either of prosecutor or plaintiffs' attorney, unless your instructor indicates a specific role. In class, you will have an office meeting. At that meeting, you will review and brainstorm your opening statement.

ASSIGNMENT 21: Defendants' Attorneys: Planning an Opening Statement

You are preparing for trial, and it is time to think about and plan your opening statement. You are aware of the importance of your opening statement. An effective opening will be the result of your trial preparation and planning.

PREPARATION

READ: (1) Trial Case File Entries 1-36, 92, 94-96, 109 (criminal case); (2) Trial Case File Entries 1-88, 92-96, 98, 109, 118 (civil case); (3) Chapter 7, *Trial Advocacy* text.

TIPS FOR THIS ASSIGNMENT

1. A good opening statement communicates the defense case theory clearly. What is your theory of the case?

   What is your case theme? What key factual points do you wish to stress?

   The words you select to convey those factual points are important. What powerful words would you select to emphasize your key points, without being argumentative?

2. The structure you use for the organization of your opening statement will determine whether the thoughts you wish to communicate are readily understood by the jury. Most trial advocates consider the narrative approach to be the best one. Why?

   Sometimes a flashback approach will work well in an opening statement. How might you use that approach in the *State v. Hard* case?

   In *Summers v. Hard*?

3. You wish to seize the jurors' attention with the introductory remarks of your opening statement. How might you begin your opening?

4. It is a well-established principle that if there is a significant weakness in your case, you should eliminate the sting during opening statement by confessing the weakness and attempting to defuse it.

   List the weak points in your case. How will you attempt to defuse those weak points in your opening statement?

5. As you think about ways to communicate with the jury, consider using visuals during your opening statement. What visuals might assist you in communicating information to the jury?

ASSIGNMENT FOR CLASS

Assume the role either of attorney for defendant Davola or attorney for defendant Hard (in *State v. Hard* or *Summers v. Hard*), according to your instructor's assignment.

In class, you will have an office meeting. At that meeting, you will review and brainstorm your opening statement.

ASSIGNMENT 22: Prosecutor, Plaintiffs', and Defendants' Attorneys: Deliver an Opening Statement

Now the court addresses the jury: "Members of the jury, will you now give your attention to counsel, who will address you in opening statement." Attorneys, it is time for you to deliver your opening statements.

PREPARATION

READ: (1) Trial Case File Entries 1-36, 92, 94-96, 109 (criminal case); (2) Trial Case File Entries 1-88, 92-96, 98, 109, 118 (civil case); (3) Chapter 7, *Trial Advocacy* text.

TIPS FOR THIS ASSIGNMENT

1. You have planned for this moment and know your opening statement by heart. There is only one last minute to run through your written checklist concerning what you intend to do during the delivery of your opening statement.

   What steps will you take to have a demeanor that is friendly, confident, and sincere?

How will you project courtesy to the court, the opposing counsel, and the jury?

2. Are the visuals you intend to use during your opening statement in place, and are they ready to be made visible to the jury?

3. Your movement in the courtroom is important. Where will you stand? When you move to another place in the courtroom, what will be your purpose in moving?

ASSIGNMENT FOR CLASS

Assume the role of prosecutor or plaintiffs' attorney or defendants' attorneys in *State v. Hard* or *Summers v. Hard*, according to your instructor's assignment. In class, present your opening statement.

Chapter 8. Exhibits and the Visual Trial

Criminal and Civil Case Assignments

ASSIGNMENT 23: Prosecutor and Plaintiffs' Attorney: Videotape of the Garage Tavern and Scene Visit (Detective Tharp)

You are contemplating whether to use a video of the Garage tavern at trial. Detective Tharp supervised the production of the videotape, which was made on September 5, 20XX.

PREPARATION

READ: (1) Trial Case File Entries 1-88, 95 (Rules 104, 401-403, 901, 1001-1004), 101, 111, 116, 122; (2) Chapter 8, *Trial Advocacy* text.

TIPS FOR THIS ASSIGNMENT

1. What is the significance of the video of the Garage tavern to your case theory? What evidentiary foundation for the videotape would you need to establish for the video's admissibility at trial?

2. Specifically, think about a jury visit to the tavern. What logistical problems do you envision?

    Imagine that your visit to the Garage convinced you it is an unsafe bar with a boisterous crowd. How could a jury visit to such a bar help the defense case theory?

    Are there any other advantages or disadvantages you can think of when you weigh a jury visit against a videotape of the Garage?

3. Assume that you have all the technology in the courtroom you need (a document camera, a projector so you can show computer images on a large screen, monitors for all the participants, presentation software). What are the possible ways you could display the video? Which would you choose for use both during witness testimony and during opening and/or closing argument?

ASSIGNMENT FOR CLASS

Assume the role of the prosecutor or plaintiffs' attorney either in *State v. Hard* or *Summers v. Hard*, according to your instructor's assignment. In class, conduct a direct examination of Detective Tharp limited to presenting the evidentiary foundation for introducing into evidence the video of the Garage tavern.

ASSIGNMENT 24: Prosecutor and Plaintiffs' Attorney: Scale Diagrams of the Garage Tavern (John Lacey, Peter Nye)

You are planning to use diagrams of the Garage tavern. During the investigation of the criminal case, the identification technician in the Ruston Police Department, John Lacey, measured the tavern and drew a nonscale diagram of it on April 1, 20XX + 1. Lacey then prepared a scale diagram on April 5, 20XX + 1. In the civil case, Peter Nye, a private investigator for plaintiffs' attorney, prepared both nonscale and scale diagrams for plaintiffs. John Lacey and Peter Nye are available to testify.

PREPARATION

READ: (1) Trial Case File Entries 1-88, 95 (Rules 104, 401-403, 901), 101, 102, 109, 122; (2) Chapter 8, *Trial Advocacy* text.

TIPS FOR THIS ASSIGNMENT

1. Explain the significance of the Garage tavern diagrams to your case theory.

2. What could you do with a scale diagram of the Garage tavern in this case that you could not do with a nonscale diagram?

   How, if at all, does the foundation for a scale diagram differ from that of a nonscale diagram?

   Who can present a foundation for this scale diagram?

3. Suppose you plan to have Deborah Summers mark the diagram. What symbols might be used to indicate the people at the tavern she illustrates on the diagram?

   If more than one witness will use the diagram, how will you be able to distinguish Deborah Summers's markings from those of another witness?

   How might you illustrate movement of people on the diagram?

   Is there any way you could show points in time on the diagram (where Deborah Summers first saw defendant Ed Hard when she entered the tavern on September 3 and where she was when she saw the shooting)?

4. Assume that you have all the technology in the courtroom you need (a document camera, a projector, a large screen that can display computer images, monitors for all the participants, presentation software). What are the possible ways you could display the diagram? Which would you choose for use both during witness testimony and during opening and/or closing argument?

ASSIGNMENT FOR CLASS

Assume the role of the prosecutor or plaintiffs' attorney either in *State v. Hard* or *Summers v. Hard*, according to your instructor's assignment. In class, conduct the direct examination of John Lacey or Peter Nye presenting the foundation for a scale diagram of the Garage tavern. Display the diagram in the most advantageous way.

ASSIGNMENT 25: Prosecutor and Plaintiffs' Attorney: Photographs of the Garage Tavern (Detective Tharp, John Lacey, Peter Nye)

You are considering the use of a series of photographs of the Garage tavern. The photographs were taken during the investigation of the criminal case by the identification technician, John Lacey, at approximately 6:00 A.M. on September 4, 20XX. In the civil case, Peter Nye, a private investigator for plaintiffs' attorney, has examined the photographs and the Garage tavern.

Detective Tharp, John Lacey, and Peter Nye are available to testify.

PREPARATION

READ: (1) Trial Case File Entries 1-88, 95 (Rules 104, 401-403, 901), 101, 102, 116, 122; (2) Chapter 8, *Trial Advocacy* text.

TIPS FOR THIS ASSIGNMENT

1. How can these photographs support your case theory?

    What foundation is required for the admission of the Garage tavern photographs?

2. If a photograph is viewed alone, it is difficult to determine the angle from which it was taken, distances from the camera lens to the object seen in the photograph, and other such matters.

    Can you relate these photographs to the diagram of the Garage to clarify the photographs during Deborah Summers's testimony?

    How could you mark the photographs and places on the diagram so that during argument or deliberation the jury (or the appellate court on review) could determine where the photographer was standing, when the picture was taken, and the angle at which the camera was pointing when the picture was taken?

3. Assume that you have all the technology in the courtroom you need (a document camera, a projector, a large screen that can display computer images, monitors for all the participants, presentation software).

    What are the possible ways you could display the photographs?

    Which would you choose for use both during witness testimony and during opening and/or closing argument?

ASSIGNMENT FOR CLASS

Assume the role of the prosecutor or plaintiffs' attorney either in *State v. Hard* or *Summers v. Hard*, according to your instructor's assignment. In class, conduct the part of the direct examination of Detective Tharp, John Lacey, or Peter Nye that will present the foundation for a series of photographs of the Garage tavern. Also, display the photographs in the most advantageous way.

ASSIGNMENT 26: Prosecutor and Plaintiffs' Attorney: Skeleton Model
(Dr. Jackson, Dr. Day)

You borrowed a model of a human skeleton from an attorney friend of yours who does a significant amount of personal injury trial work. You want to illustrate Dr. Jackson's or Dr. Day's testimony regarding Bruno Summers's fatal wounds using the model.

PREPARATION

READ: (1) Trial Case File Entries 1-88, 95 (Rules 104, 401-403, 901), 111, 116, 122 (criminal and civil cases); (2) Chapter 8 (criminal and civil cases), *Trial Advocacy* text.

TIPS FOR THIS ASSIGNMENT

1. Generally, what part of the doctor's testimony will be enriched by using the skeletal model? What specific impact do you want the skeletal model to have on the jury?

   What foundation is necessary to use the skeletal model to illustrate the doctors' testimony?

2. Will the skeletal model become an exhibit (marked for identification, sent to the jury room, and then, on conviction, retained by the county clerk)?

   Think about this scenario: You offer the skeletal model for illustrative purposes only, but defense counsel requests that it be marked and admitted into evidence if the jury is to consider it. What would be your response?

3. Assume that you have all the technology in the courtroom you need (a document camera, a projector so you can show computer images on a large screen, monitors for all the participants, presentation software).

What are the possible ways you could display the skeleton model? Which would you choose for use both during witness testimony and during opening and/or closing argument?

ASSIGNMENT FOR CLASS

Assume the role of the prosecutor or plaintiffs' attorney either in *State v. Hard* or *Summers v. Hard*, according to your instructor's assignment. In class, prosecutor, prepare to conduct the direct examination of the medical examiner, Dr. Jackson.

Plaintiffs' attorney, prepare to conduct the direct examination of Dr. Day, Bruno's treating physician at Mercy Hospital.

Testimony for both witnesses should (a) establish the foundation for admissibility of the skeletal model and (b) illustrate, by use of the model or other substitute visual, the doctors' testimony as to the fatal wounds to Bruno Summers.

ASSIGNMENT 27: Prosecutor and Plaintiffs' Attorney: Hospital Records of Bruno Summers
(Rose Gadfly)

You are ready to offer Bruno Summers's hospital records into evidence. Keep in mind that these records present at least two levels of hearsay. You must satisfy each level for admission. Rose Gadfly, chief records clerk at Mercy Hospital, is available to testify.

PREPARATION

READ: (1) Trial Case File Entries 1-88, 95 (Rules 104, 401-403, 803, 901, 902, 1001-1004), 101, 122; (2) Chapter 8, *Trial Advocacy* text.

TIPS FOR THIS ASSIGNMENT

1. Explain the significance of the hospital records to your theory of the case.

2. What foundation is necessary for the admission into evidence of the hospital records of Bruno Summers?

    Which witnesses can present the foundation for the Bruno Summers's hospital records?

3. List any evidentiary problems other than foundation problems that you might encounter in trying to admit the hospital records into evidence. How will you deal with them?

4. Assume that you have all the technology in the courtroom you need (a document camera, a projector so you can show computer images on a large screen, monitors for all the participants, presentation software).

    What are the possible ways you could display the hospital records? Which would you choose for use both during witness testimony and during opening and/or closing argument?

ASSIGNMENT FOR CLASS

Assume the role of the prosecutor or plaintiffs' attorney either in *State v. Hard* or *Summers v. Hard*, according to your instructor's assignment. In class, conduct the examination of Rose Gadfly, chief records clerk at Mercy Hospital, in order to have Bruno's hospital records admitted into evidence. Display the records in the most advantageous way.

ASSIGNMENT 28: Prosecutor and Plaintiffs' Attorney: Weapons Applications and Check
(Fred Faye)

On August 27, at 1:30 P.M., Defendant Edward Hard purchased from the American Gun Shop the .22-caliber revolver used to kill Bruno Summers. To prove this, you want to offer into evidence the Application to Transfer Pistol or Revolver, the Firearms Transaction Record, and the check to the American Gun Shop. These documents are purportedly signed by Edward T. Hard.

Fred Faye, the American Gun Shop owner, is available to testify regarding these documents. Fred Faye saw the defendant sign the application, the transaction record, and the check. A handwriting expert, Virginia Johnson, compared the signature on the documents with a handwriting exemplar prepared by the defendant in her presence. In Ms. Johnson's opinion, based on the handwriting comparison, Edward Hard signed the documents.

PREPARATION

READ: (1) Trial Case File Entries 1-72, 74-88, 95 (Rules 104, 401-403, 609, 803, 901, 902, 1001-1004), 100, 101, 112, 122 (civil and criminal cases); (2) Trial Case File Entry 73 (civil case only); (3) Chapter 8, *Trial Advocacy* text.

TIPS FOR THIS ASSIGNMENT

1. Explain the significance of the application, the transaction record, and the check to your theory of the case.

    How do you plan on using the documents during the trial?

2. You need to consider how to present the foundation for the admissibility of the documents.

    Which witnesses can provide the foundation for the admissibility of these exhibits?

    Describe all the ways in which a foundation for the admissibility of these documents could be established.

3. Assume that you have all the technology in the courtroom you need (a document camera, a projector so you can show computer images on a large screen, monitors for all the participants, presentation software).

    What are the possible ways you would display the weapons applications and check?

    Which would you choose for use both during witness testimony and during opening?

    Closing argument?

ASSIGNMENT FOR CLASS

Assume the role of the prosecutor or plaintiffs' attorney either in *State v. Hard* or *Summers v. Hard*, according to your instructor's assignment. In class, conduct an examination of Fred Faye in order to have the documents admitted into evidence. Also, display the documents in the most advantageous way.

ASSIGNMENT 29: Attorney for Defendant Hard: Scale Diagram of the Gas Station
(John Gooding)

You want John Gooding to use a scale diagram of the Gull gas station to illustrate his testimony about the gas station incident on August 26, 20XX, in which Bruno Summers allegedly threatened Ed Hard's life. You also want John Gooding to present the foundation for the diagram of the gas station.

A private investigator for Ed Hard went to the gas station and measured it. She also inquired and found out that the gas station was in exactly the same condition on August 26 as it was on November 8, 20XX. A scale diagram of the gas station was prepared by the defense investigator on November 8, 20XX.

PREPARATION

READ: (1) Trial Case File Entries 1-74, 76-88, 95 (Rules 104, 401-403, 901), 101, 109, 122 (civil and criminal cases); (2) Trial Case File Entry 75 (civil case only); (3) Chapter 8, *Trial Advocacy* text.

TIPS FOR THIS ASSIGNMENT

1. Generally, explain the significance of the gas station diagram to the defense case theory. What part of Gooding's testimony will be aided by a scale diagram?

2. Can John Gooding provide the foundation for the scale diagram? If not, does that mean he cannot use the diagram at all?

   What objection might plaintiffs make to such a use of the diagram?

3. Assume that you have all the technology in the courtroom you need (a document camera, a projector so you can show computer images on a large screen, monitors for all the participants, presentation software).

   What are the possible ways you could display the scale diagram?

   Which would you choose for use both during witness testimony and during opening?

   Closing argument?

ASSIGNMENT FOR CLASS

Assume the role of defendant Hard's defense counsel either in *State v. Hard* or *Summers v. Hard*, according to your instructor's assignment. In class, conduct the direct examination of John Gooding in which you will present the foundation for the admissibility of the diagram and illustrate his testimony by using the scale diagram of the gas station.

ASSIGNMENT 30: Attorney for Defendant Hard: Neo-Nazi Membership Card *(Officer West, Rebecca Karr, Nurse Frank)*

Bruno Summers's neo-Nazi membership card was obtained by Officer West at the same time that the officer obtained Bruno Summers's clothes. Specifically, Nurse Frank was on duty in the emergency room at Mercy Hospital the night of September 3 when Bruno Summers was brought into the emergency room. She removed his clothes and possessions and put them in a plastic basin at the end of the gurney.

Officer West arrived at the hospital at approximately 10:30 P.M. The officer entered the emergency room and requested Bruno Summers's clothing and possessions. Nurse Frank gave Officer West the plastic basin that was at the end of the gurney.

Officer West left the hospital and went to the evidence room at the police department. Officer West then individually tagged the items that were removed from the basin with Bruno Summers's name and a police file number. In a wallet taken from a pocket of Bruno's trousers, West found a neo-Nazi membership card. The items were then entered in the evidence book. To obtain the evidence, an officer must sign the evidence out in the evidence book and note the date, time, and destination.

In the period prior to the fatal shooting, Rebecca Karr, a friend of Ed Hard's, attended meetings of the neo-Nazi survivalist group that Bruno Summers belonged to. Although she attended the group meetings only a few times, she is able to identify the symbol on the neo-Nazi membership card because it is the same symbol that was on a poster at the survivalist meeting.

You have made an enlargement of the neo-Nazi card.

PREPARATION

READ: (1) Trial Case File Entries 1-77, 79-88, 95 (Rules 104, 401-403, 404, 801, 803, 901, 1001-1004), 100-102, 122 (criminal and civil cases); (2) Trial Case File Entry 78 (civil case only); (3) Chapter 8, *Trial Advocacy* text.

TIPS FOR THIS ASSIGNMENT

1. If there is testimony that Bruno Summers was an active member of a neo-Nazi survivalist group, why do you want the membership card in evidence to support your case theory?

   How will you use the membership card during the trial?

   What foundation is necessary for its admission? Which witnesses will you need?

2. Will you need testimony of all three witnesses to tell a complete narrative about these pieces of evidence?

3. Assume that you have all the technology in the courtroom you need (a document camera, a projector so you can show computer images on a large screen, monitors for all the participants, presentation software).

   What are the possible ways you would display the neo-Nazi membership card?

   Which would you choose for use both during witness testimony and during opening?

   Closing argument?

ASSIGNMENT FOR CLASS

Assume the role of defendant Hard's defense counsel either in *State v. Hard* or *Summers v. Hard*, according to your instructor's assignment. In class, conduct the part of the direct examination of Officer West, Nurse Frank, and/or Rebecca Karr that will present the foundation for admission of the neo-Nazi membership card into evidence and illustrate Officer West's, Nurse Frank's, and/or Rebecca Karr's testimony by using the neo-Nazi card. Display the card in the most advantageous way.

ASSIGNMENT 31: Attorneys for Defendants Hard and Davola: Death Certificate
(Dr. Day, Dr. Jackson)

Dr. Brett Day was the doctor who attended Bruno Summers until he died. Dr. L.R. Jackson, the medical examiner, signed the death certificate. Both doctors are available to testify.

PREPARATION

READ: (1) Trial Case File Entries 1-70, 72-88, 95 (Rules 104, 401-403, 803, 901, 902, 1001-1005), 101, 122 (criminal and civil cases); (2) Trial Case File Entry 71 (civil case only); (3) Chapter 8, *Trial Advocacy* text.

TIPS FOR THIS ASSIGNMENT

1. Why do you want the death certificate admitted into evidence to support your case theory?

   How will you use the death certificate during the trial?

2. Think about the evidentiary foundation for admission of a death certificate into evidence.

   Can the death certificate be admitted into evidence without calling any witnesses?

3. Both Dr. Jackson and Dr. Day are available to testify. They can testify to facts and opinion, but can either one or both of them establish a foundation for admissibility of the death certificate?

   If you were able to qualify the death certificate as a public record, are all the entries on the certificate admitted?

4. Assume that you have all the technology in the courtroom you need (a document camera, a projector so you can show computer images on a large screen, monitors for all the participants, presentation software).

   What are the possible ways you could display the death certificate?

   Which would you choose for use both during witness testimony and during opening?

   Closing argument?

ASSIGNMENT FOR CLASS

Assume the role either of attorney for defendant Hard or attorney for defendant Davola in *State v. Hard* or *Summers v. Hard*, according to your instructor's assignment. In class, conduct the part of the examination of Dr. Jackson or Dr. Day that will present the foundation to admit the death certificate into evidence. Display the certificate in the most advantageous way.

ASSIGNMENT 32: Attorney for Defendant Hard: Bruno Summers's Knife
(Officer West, Nurse Frank)

You would like Bruno Summers's knife admitted into evidence. Two witnesses are available: Officer West and Nurse Frank. Specifically, Nurse Frank was on duty in the emergency room at Mercy Hospital the night of September 3 when Bruno Summers was brought into the emergency room. She removed his clothes and put them in a plastic basin at the end of the gurney. Nurse Frank found a knife in a closed position in Bruno Summers's jacket pocket.

Officer West arrived at the hospital at approximately 10:30 P.M. She entered the emergency room and requested Bruno Summers's clothing and possessions. Nurse Frank gave Officer West the plastic basin that was at the end of the gurney.

Officer West left the hospital and went to the evidence room at the police department. There Officer West individually tagged the items that were removed from the basin with Bruno Summers's name and a police file number. One of those tagged items was the knife. The items were then entered in the evidence book. To obtain the evidence, an officer must sign the evidence out in the evidence book and note the date, time, and destination. Officer West listed the knife as Item 3 on the evidence record in the police report, (Case File Entry 4).

PREPARATION

READ: (1) Trial Case File Entries 1-70, 72-88, 94, 95 (Rules 104, 401-403, 404, 901), 100-102, 122 (criminal and civil cases); (2) Trial Case File Entry 71 (civil case only); (3) Chapter 8, *Trial Advocacy* text.

TIPS FOR THIS ASSIGNMENT

1. What is the significance of Bruno Summers's knife to your theory of the case?

   How will you argue in closing argument concerning the knife's presence in Bruno's pocket?

2. Plan to present an evidentiary foundation for admissibility of the knife. How will you establish that the knife in court is the same one found by Nurse Frank and given to Officer West on the night of the shooting?

   Do you anticipate any evidentiary problems in trying to have the knife admitted into evidence? How will you deal with them?

3. Assume that you have all the technology in the courtroom you need (a document camera, a projector so you can show computer images on a large screen, monitors for all the participants, presentation software).

    What are the possible ways you could display the knife? Which would you choose for use both during witness testimony and during opening?

    Closing argument?

ASSIGNMENT FOR CLASS

Assume the role of defense counsel either in *State v. Hard* or *Summers v. Hard*, according to your instructor's assignment. In class, conduct the part of the direct examination of Officer West and/or Nurse Frank that establishes the foundation for introducing into evidence Bruno Summers's knife. Display the knife in the most advantageous way.

ASSIGNMENT 33: Prosecutor and Plaintiffs' Attorney: Cross-Examination with a Prior Written Statement and Prior Conviction
(Ed Hard)

You plan on using two items of documentary evidence during the cross-examination of the defendant, Ed Hard: (1) his September 3 written statement and (2) his prior conviction documents. Imagine for this problem only that during Hard's direct examination, he testified to the following facts: He noticed Bruno Summers the moment Bruno entered the Garage tavern on September 3.

On September 3, while Ed Hard was in the tavern, Bruno Summers never touched him.

Imagine for this problem only that the court has made pretrial rulings as follows:

- Defendant's written statement to Detective Tharp on September 3 at 11:30 P.M. was voluntarily made but will be inadmissible during the prosecutor (or plaintiffs') case-in-chief. However, it may be admissible as a prior inconsistent statement of Ed Hard if he were to testify.

- Ed Hard has a May 19, 20XX - 6 conviction in Ruston, Major, for taking and riding a motor vehicle without permission of the owner. During pretrial, the court denied the defendant's motion in limine and held the conviction is admissible to affect the credibility of the defendant

Hard if he were to testify. It is inadmissible for any other purpose. The court ruled only on admissibility of a prior conviction to impeach the credibility of a witness.

PREPARATION

READ: (1) Trial Case File Entries 10, 12, 95 (Rules 104, 401-403, 609, 613, 801, 803, 901, 902, 1001-1004), 112, 122 (criminal and civil cases); (2) Trial Case File Entry 76 (civil case only); (3) Chapter 8, *Trial Advocacy* text.

TIPS FOR THIS ASSIGNMENT

1. Concerning the defendant's prior written statement:

    What is the significance of the defendant's prior statement to your case theory?

    What foundation is necessary for the prior statement to be admissible during cross-examination?

2. As prosecutor or plaintiffs' attorney, how might the defendant respond to your cross-examination about the prior written statement?

    Now suppose the defendant admits making inconsistent statements in his statement of September 3. How would he respond?

3. Now, concerning the defendant's prior conviction, what foundation is necessary for the prior conviction to be admissible during cross-examination?

ASSIGNMENT FOR CLASS

Assume the role of prosecutor or plaintiffs' attorney in *State v. Hard* or *Summers v. Hard*, according to your instructor's assignment. In class, conduct the cross-examination of Edward Hard, presenting a foundation for admissibility of Ed Hard's prior written statement dated September 3 and his prior conviction.

ASSIGNMENT 34: Attorney for Defendant Hard: Bruno Summers's Blood Sample (*Officer Harris*)

You have subpoenaed one witness, Officer Harris, concerning the blood specimen. Dr. Brett Day took the blood specimen from Bruno Summers at Mercy

Hospital at approximately 11:00 P.M. on September 3, 20XX. He labeled the specimen showing the time, the amount collected, and the patient's name and medical number. The blood specimen was then placed in the laboratory refrigerator. On September 4, 20XX, Dr. Day removed the blood specimen from the laboratory refrigerator and gave it to Officer Harris. Officer Harris placed the blood in a dry ice container and transported the blood specimen by police patrol car to the evidence room of the Ruston Police Department. Officer Harris tagged the sample and placed it in the evidence room refrigerator.

On September 4, 20XX, at 5:00 P.M. Officer Harris set off to deliver the blood specimen (again packed in dry ice) to the State of Major Toxicology Laboratory for analysis. On the way to the laboratory, Officer Harris stopped for dinner. He left the evidence in the back seat of his patrol car. He might have left his car door unlocked. Officer Harris then delivered the blood specimen to the Toxicology Laboratory to Dr. Daisys, a state toxicologist, who analyzed the blood for its blood alcohol level and later issued a report to Dorian R. Flannery, who assisted Dr. Jackson with the autopsy. This report is included in the medical examiner's report. Dr. Daisys is not available to testify. Officer Harris returned the specimen to the evidence room at 9:00 P.M. on September 4 and logged it in the evidence book. Officer Hams listed the sample in the evidence record in the police report as Item 9.

PREPARATION

READ: (1) Trial Case File Entries 1-88, 94, 95 (Rules 104, 401-403, 404, 803, 901, 902, 1001-1004), 101, 122; (2) Chapter 8, *Trial Advocacy* text.

TIPS FOR THIS ASSIGNMENT

1. Is the blood specimen testimony concerning the alcohol level in Bruno's body relevant to your case theory?

2. How will you establish that the sample in court is the same one that was taken from Bruno at the hospital?

   Which witnesses can you use?

   Do you anticipate any evidentiary problems in trying to have the blood sample admitted into evidence? How will you deal with them?

3. Assume that you have all the technology in the courtroom you need (a document camera, a projector so you can show computer images on a large screen, monitors for all the participants, presentation software).

What are the possible ways you could display the blood sample? Which would you choose for use both during witness testimony and during opening and/or closing argument?

ASSIGNMENT FOR CLASS

Assume the role of defense attorney either in *State v. Hard* or *Summers v. Hard*, according to your instructor's assignment. In class, conduct the part of the direct examination of Officer Harris that will establish part of the foundation for introducing into evidence the blood sample. Display the blood sample in the most advantageous way.

ASSIGNMENT 35: Attorney for Defendant Hard:
Courtroom Demonstration
(Ed Hard)

As you plan the direct examination of defendant Ed Hard, you are considering a courtroom demonstration. Specifically, you are thinking about having Hard demonstrate how Bruno Summers approached him from behind on August 26 at the Gull gas station and placed a knife to his side.

PREPARATION

READ: (1) Trial Case File Entries 1-75, 77-88, 95 (Rules 104, 401-403), 102, 122 (criminal and civil cases); (2) Trial Case File Entry 76 (civil case only); (3) Chapter 8, *Trial Advocacy* text.

TIPS FOR THIS ASSIGNMENT

1. What objective are you attempting to accomplish by having the defendant do a courtroom demonstration of the incident of August 26?

2. What out-of-court preparation would you engage in with the defendant before ever embarking on an in-court demonstration?

   Who would you plan on using as participants in the in-court demonstration?

3. If you attempted to use Bruno Summers's knife, which defendant Hard cannot identify as the knife that was used on August 26, what objections do you anticipate that opposing counsel might make?

How would you respond to the anticipated objections by the prosecutor or plaintiffs' counsel to the use of Bruno Summers's knife during the courtroom demonstration?

4. What, if any, ethical concerns do you have regarding the use of Bruno Summers's knife in the demonstration?

ASSIGNMENT FOR CLASS

Assume the role of defense attorney either in *State v. Hard* or *Summers v. Hard*, according to your instructor's assignment. In class, conduct the part of the direct examination of the defendant, Ed Hard, in which you present a courtroom demonstration.

Criminal Case Assignments

ASSIGNMENT 36: Prosecutor: Gun, Rounds, and Slugs (*Officer Yale, Officer Harris, H. Tredwell*)

Your goal is to prove the slug recovered from Bruno Summers's body was fired from the gun recovered from Ed Hard's residence. To achieve this result, you need the following exhibits admitted into evidence: the .22-caliber revolver, the four live rounds and one expended round, the slug taken from Bruno Summers's body, and the test slug that firearms examiner Tredwell fired from that .22-caliber revolver and compared with the slug recovered from Bruno Summers's body.

Officer Yale arrived at Ed Hard's house at approximately 10:30 P.M. on September 3, 20XX. He retrieved a .22-caliber revolver from Ed Hard's living room. The revolver had four live rounds of ammunition and one spent round in it. Officer Yale took these items to the police evidence room, where he tagged the revolver and packaged it in a sealed bag and put the rounds in another sealed bag, which he also tagged. On each tag, he wrote his name, the police case number, and a police evidence number (gun, Item 5; rounds, Item 6). He noted these items in the police evidence record for the police report.

Bruno Summers, after arriving at Mercy Hospital, was examined in the emergency room and then transferred to surgery for removal of the bullet. Dr. Brett Day, the head of the surgery team, found a bullet lodged in Summers's chest wall, embedded in the interior/superior aspect of the eighth rib. Dr. Day removed the bullet and placed it in a plastic envelope. The attending nurse, Betty Frank, labeled and sealed the envelope and returned it to Dr. Day. Dr. Day put the envelope in his locked desk drawer. On September 4, 20XX, at 2:30 P.M. Officer Harris from the Ruston Police Department collected the slug in the sealed envelope (along with the blood sample) from Dr. Day. The officer delivered the evidence to the police evidence room, where Harris tagged it with Bruno Summers's name, his own initials, and the case file number. The evidence was then logged into the evidence record book.

Tredwell can provide expert testimony about the gun and the firearms comparison of the slug that he test-fired with the slug recovered from Bruno Summers's body. Firearms examiner Tredwell signed out the slug as well as the revolver, four live rounds, and one spent one from the evidence room and took them to the crime laboratory for inspection and tests. Mr. Tredwell kept them in his safe when they were not being used for tests. After Tredwell completed his tests, he returned the evidence, including the test-fired slug (which he sealed in a small envelope), to the police evidence room and logged each item into the record book.

PREPARATION

READ: (1) Trial Case File Entries 1-88, 95 (Rules 104, 401-403, 901), 101, 122; (2) Chapter 8, *Trial Advocacy* text.

TIPS FOR THIS ASSIGNMENT

1. What is the significance of the .22-caliber revolver? The four live rounds? The expended round recovered from Ed Hard's house to your theory of the case?

2. Think about establishing the foundation for admissibility of the .22-caliber revolver, the four live rounds, and the expended round recovered from Ed Hard's house. How will you establish that the gun seized by Officer Yale is the same gun tested by H. Tredwell? How will you establish that the gun seized by Officer Yale is the same gun that is in court?

3. What is the significance of the test-fired slug to your case theory?

4. Plan how you will present a foundation for the admissibility of the slug test-fired from the .22-caliber revolver by H. Tredwell. Consider how you will establish the necessary chain of custody: How will you establish that the test-fired slug is the same slug that is in court?

5. Assume that you have all the technology in the courtroom you need (a document camera, a projector so you can show computer images on a large screen, monitors for all the participants, presentation software).

What are the possible ways you could display the slug, the revolver, the ammunition, and the test-fired slug?

Which would you choose for use both during witness testimony and during opening and/or closing argument?

ASSIGNMENT FOR CLASS

In class, conduct the direct examination of Officer Yale, Officer Harris, and H. Tredwell, presenting a foundation for admissibility of the slug, the revolver, the ammunition, and the test-fired slug. Display the gun, rounds, and slugs in the most advantageous ways. You may assume that you have established the chain of custody of the slug from Dr. Day to Officer Harris.

Civil Case Assignments

ASSIGNMENT 37: Plaintiffs' Attorney: Photographs *(Deborah Summers)*

You are considering using family photographs during the direct examination of Deborah Summers, and you believe these photographs will aid the jury in understanding Deborah Summers's testimony.

These family photographs were taken on Christmas Day 20XX-1 and in August 20XX at a picnic. No one can remember who took any of these photographs or any of the technical details.

Additionally, photographs of Bruno Summers and of Bruno and Deborah Summers were taken by Peter Dean right after the shooting in the Garage tavern. No one who took any of these photographs is available to testify.

PREPARATION

READ: (1) Trial Case File Entries 1-88, 95 (Rules 104, 401-403, 901), 102, 111, 122; (2) Chapter 8, *Trial Advocacy* text.

TIPS FOR THIS ASSIGNMENT

1. What is the significance of these photographs to plaintiffs' case theory? What part of Deborah Summers's testimony will be aided by photographs?

2. What foundation is required in Deborah Summers's testimony for the admissibility of the photographs?

3. Now you must plan to meet defense trial strategies. Think about this defense strategy: In conjunction with the defense motion to exclude all the photographs, the defense offers to stipulate that Deborah, Amanda, and Ronnie were a happy family, celebrated holidays together, and enjoyed family outings, that Bruno Summers will be missed by his family.

    What effect does the offer to stipulate have on your arguments in favor of the admissibility of the photographs? Must you accept the stipulation?

    Would you accept the stipulation?

4. Imagine the court has ruled on the defense motion in limine as follows: One photograph of Bruno Summers lying on the floor is admissible; you are prohibited from using the rest. During direct examination of Deborah Summers, defense counsel indicates to the court that the defense has a motion and asks that the jury be excused while the motion is presented. In the jury's absence, defense counsel moves for a mistrial on the basis that you have deliberately and unethically shown the jury the photograph of Deborah and Bruno. You look down and see that one of the excluded photographs has slipped from your trial file and is partly exposed to view at counsel table. This was not deliberate on your part, and you doubt the jury could see the photograph since it is flat on the table and several feet from the jury.

    How would you respond to the motion for mistrial and the argument that you acted unethically?

5. Assume that you have all the technology in the courtroom you need (a document camera, a projector so you can show computer images on a large screen, monitors for all the participants, presentation software).

    What are the possible ways you could display the photographs? Which would you choose for use both during witness testimony and during opening?

    Closing argument?

ASSIGNMENT FOR CLASS

In class, conduct the part of the direct examination of Deborah Summers in which you will present the foundations for admissibility of the photographs and use the photographs to illustrate her testimony. Display the photographs in the most advantageous way.

ASSIGNMENT 38: Plaintiffs' Attorney: Hospital, Ambulance, and Funeral Bills
(Deborah and Hans Summers, Rose Gadfly)

You would like to introduce into evidence the hospital, ambulance, and funeral bills of Bruno Summers. Three witnesses are available: Deborah Summers, Hans Summers, and Rose Gadfly, hospital records clerk and bookkeeper.

PREPARATION

READ: (1) Trial Case File Entries 1-88, 95 (Rules 104, 401-403, 801-803, 901), 122; (2) Chapter 8, *Trial Advocacy* text.

TIPS FOR THIS ASSIGNMENT

1. Suppose Deborah Summers and one of the administrators of Bruno's estate, Hans Summers, testify about the sum total of the bills and what has been paid. Why do you need to introduce these bills into evidence? How will you use the bills?

2. What foundation is necessary for the admission of the bills? Which witnesses can present the foundation for the bills?

3. Assume that you have all the technology in the courtroom you need (a document camera, a projector so you can show computer images on a large screen, monitors for all the participants, presentation software).

    What are the possible ways you could display the hospital, ambulance, and funeral bills?

    Which would you choose for use both during witness testimony and during opening?

    Closing argument?

ASSIGNMENT FOR CLASS

In class, conduct the examination of any or all of the following witnesses according to your instructor's assignment: (a) Deborah Summers, (b) Hans Summers, (c) Rose Gadfly. Establish through these witnesses' testimony the foundation for admission of the hospital, ambulance, and funeral bills into evidence. Display the bills in the most advantageous way.

ASSIGNMENT 39: Attorney for Defendant Hard: Medical Records of Deborah Summers (*Dr. Sherman Croup*)

The Neva County clinic medical records were prepared by Dr. Sherman Croup. Dr. Croup has a family practice and works at Neva County Medical Services Clinic in Ruston. In this capacity, he examined Deborah Summers in October 20XX; he diagnosed her as a mild hysteric and decided not to refill her prescription for Valium. Dr. Croup is available to testify. You would like to have the court admit the Neva clinic medical records.

PREPARATION

READ: (1) Trial Case File Entries 1-88, 95 (Rules 104, 401-403, 404, 801-803, 901, 902, 1001-1004), 122; (2) Chapter 8, *Trial Advocacy* text.

TIPS FOR THIS ASSIGNMENT

1. Explain the significance of the clinic records prepared by Dr. Croup to your theory of the case.

2. What foundation is necessary for the admission into evidence of Deborah Summers's clinic records?

    Which witnesses can present the foundation for the clinic records of Deborah Summers?

3. Assume that you have all the technology in the courtroom you need (a document camera, a projector so you can show computer images on a large screen, monitors for all the participants, presentation software).

    What are the possible ways you could display the medical records? Which would you choose for use both during witness testimony and during opening?

    Closing argument?

ASSIGNMENT FOR CLASS

In class, conduct the examination of Dr. Croup to have Deborah's clinic medical records admitted into evidence. Display the records in the most advantageous way.

Chapter 9. Direct Examination: Building the Case

Criminal Case Assignments

ASSIGNMENT 40: Defense Attorney: Preparation of Direct Examination *(John Gooding)*

John Gooding, a close friend of Ed Hard's, was with Ed at the Garage tavern on August 20 and September 3 and at the Gull gas station on August 26. You should prepare John Gooding for his testimony.

PREPARATION

READ: (1) Trial Case File Entries 1-88, 94, 95 (Rules 404, 405, 607, 608, 803), 96, 97, 99-101, 111; (2) Chapter 9, *Trial Advocacy* text.

TIPS FOR THIS ASSIGNMENT

1.   Preparation includes determining what testimony you may elicit that supports your case theory and also anticipating opposing counsel's cross-examination so you can possibly defuse it during your direct examination.

     What objectives would you attempt to accomplish when preparing John Gooding for direct examination? What do you gain by character testimony? Is it worth it?

     Is there a danger that if Gooding's character testimony is vulnerable to cross-examination, it will discredit the rest of his testimony?

2.   What factual points do you wish to prepare John Gooding to present on direct examination that support your case theory?

3.   Ed Hard has insisted that John Gooding should present character evidence that Hard has a reputation for being peaceful and that Bruno Summers had a reputation for violence and a history of violent and aggressive acts. Is there an evidentiary rationale for the admission of how will you prepare Gooding to present Hard's reputation for peacefulness? How will you prepare Gooding to present Bruno's history of violent and aggressive acts?

4.   Suppose John Gooding states: "I'll do anything I can to help Ed Hard." How will you respond to this, if at all? Why?

ASSIGNMENT FOR CLASS

In class, meet with and prepare John Gooding for his direct examination. Plan to use documentary, demonstrative, and/or real evidence unless your instructor indicates otherwise.

ASSIGNMENT 41: Prosecutor: Direct Examination of Fred Faye

Fred Faye, the American Gun Shop owner, is your third witness. Deborah Summers and Peter Dean have already testified. Faye allegedly sold the fatal revolver to Ed Hard between the time of the first incident at the Garage on August 20, 20XX, and the shooting on September 3, 20XX. Mr. Faye has the dealer's copies of the Transfer Pistol or Revolver and the Firearms Transaction Record, which bear the serial number of the weapon and the written signature, "Edward Taylor Hard." He also has a copy of a canceled check bearing the same signature—"Edward Taylor Hard"—with a file stamp on the photocopy dated August 27, 20XX.

The Application to Transfer Pistol or Revolver, the Firearms Transaction Record, and the file-stamped copy of the check may assist you in establishing the dates and facts relevant to the gun purchase.

PREPARATION

READ: (1) Trial Case File Entries 1-36, 91, 94, 95 (Rules 404, 609, 803, 901, 902, 1001-1004), 96, 97, 99-102, 111, 122; (2) Chapter 9, *Trial Advocacy* text.

TIPS FOR THIS ASSIGNMENT

1. What objectives do you plan on achieving through your direct examination of Fred Faye? As with all documents, you must be aware of the necessary evidentiary foundation for their admissibility.

2. What is the relevance of Mr. Faye's testimony about the gun purchase to your legal theory of the case? Factual theory of the case?

3. Which factual points do you wish to present in Fred Faye's direct examination? If you can prove that Ed Hard used the revolver?

   Why do you also want to prove the circumstances under which Hard acquired the gun?

   What will be the likely defense response to Faye's testimony?

ASSIGNMENT FOR CLASS

In class, conduct the direct and redirect examination of Fred Faye, including questions about (a) Fred Faye's background, (b) Application to Transfer Pistol or Revolver c) the Firearms Transaction Record and (d) the copy of the canceled check. Plan to use documentary, demonstrative, and/or real evidence unless your instructor indicates otherwise.

ASSIGNMENT 42: Prosecutor: Direct Examination of Cindy Rigg

Your case-in-chief is well under way; you have called three witnesses, Deborah Summers, Peter Dean, and Fred Faye. Now you wish to focus the jury's attention on August 20. As your next witness, you call Cindy Rigg, a patron in the tavern that night, who saw the fight between Edward Hard and Bruno Summers.

PREPARATION

READ: (1) Trial Case File Entries 1-46, 91, 94, 95 (Rules 401-403, 404, 803), 96, 97, 99-102, 111; (2) Chapter 9, *Trial Advocacy* text.

TIPS FOR THIS ASSIGNMENT

1. What objectives do you plan to accomplish during the direct examination of Cindy Rigg?

   How, specifically, does Cindy Rigg's testimony help your theory of the case?

2. Think about the interplay between the testimony of the different witnesses. You have already called Deborah Summers, who testified about the fight on August 20.

   Why would you call Cindy Rigg to testify about the same subject?

   What reasons exist not to call Cindy Rigg as a witness?

3. Imagine that defense counsel on cross-examination mentioned Cindy Rigg's written witness statement but went no further with it (trying to leave the impression with the jury that she said something inconsistent with her testimony).

What, if any, ethical problems might exist if on redirect examination you offer the statement as an exhibit, knowing it would be objected to as hearsay and the judge would probably sustain the objection?

ASSIGNMENT FOR CLASS

In class, conduct the direct and redirect examination of Cindy Rigg. Plan to use documentary, demonstrative, and/or real evidence unless your instructor indicates otherwise.

ASSIGNMENT 43: Prosecutor: Direct Examination of Roberta Montbank

You are going to call Roberta Montbank to testify. Ms. Montbank was an eyewitness to the shooting on September 3, 20XX, at the Garage tavern. The police mistakenly understood her name was Robin Luntlebunk and thus could not find her. But an investigator for EKKO, the insurance company for Davola, the tavern owner, located Ms. Montbank and took her statement on October 26, 20XX. On November 3, 20XX, she gave a witness statement to the police.

The diagram and photographs of the Garage tavern have already been admitted into evidence. Witnesses you have already called to testify are Deborah Summers, Peter Dean, Fred Faye, and Cindy Rigg.

PREPARATION

READ: (1) Trial Case File Entries 1-36, 87, 95 (Rules 401-403, 601, 612, 803), 96, 97, 99, 101, 102, 111, 117; (2) Chapter 9, *Trial Advocacy* text.

TIPS FOR THIS ASSIGNMENT

1. What objectives do you plan to achieve through your direct examination of Roberta Montbank? A word of caution: Roberta's testimony is as fraught with difficulties as it is important to your case.

    What are the difficulties?

2. Imagine that during direct examination Ms. Montbank cannot remember where she sat in the Garage tavern on September 3, 20XX. What will you do?

    Suppose that you show her the signed statement she gave to the police, and it does not refresh her recollection. What will you do?

Even if Roberta Montbank's statement is read to the jury, how, if at all, can you avoid also giving the jury information that Ms. Montbank has a failing memory and, perhaps, generally poor perceptual abilities?

Should you attempt to avoid offering this information about her failing memory to the jury?

3. What problems do you anticipate Roberta Montbank will face on cross-examination? How do you plan to deal with them?

ASSIGNMENT FOR CLASS

In class, conduct the direct examination of Roberta Montbank. Have her use photographs and a diagram of the Garage, which have already been admitted into evidence, to illustrate her testimony. Plan to use documentary, demonstrative, and/or real evidence unless your instructor indicates otherwise.

ASSIGNMENT 44: Prosecutor: Direct Examination of Officer Yale
(Breathalyzer Test; Alcohol Influence Report; Opinion)

Officer Yale arrested defendant Hard and seized a .22 caliber revolver containing four live rounds and one expended round. Between midnight and 1:00 A.M. on September 4, 20XX, Officer Yale completed the Alcohol Influence Report. Yale had Ed Hard perform physical tests for intoxication, and then conducted a breathalyzer test on Ed Hard that registered a reading of .16.

Thus far in your case-in-chief, you have called all the lay witnesses and Officer West. Assume the court has determined that the search and seizure of the revolver were proper and that Ed Hard's statements to Officer Yale are admissible. The revolver, four rounds, and one bullet casing are in evidence. The Alcohol Influence Report has not yet been admitted into evidence.

PREPARATION

READ: (1) Trial Case File Entries 1-36, 87, 95 (Rules 401-403, 701-705, 803, 901), 96, 97, 101, 102, 110; (2) Chapter 9, *Trial Advocacy* text.

TIPS FOR THIS ASSIGNMENT

1. What objectives do you intend to accomplish during your direct examination of Officer Yale?

How would the breathalyzer reading help support your case theory?

Specifically, how is the breathalyzer reading relevant to the case?

2. You plan to offer the breathalyzer reading during Officer Yale's direct examination. Do you think the defense will object to its admission?

   How might the defense use the .16 breathalyzer reading to its advantage in closing argument? If the defense wished to argue that Ed Hard was sober at the time he shot Bruno Summers, which facts could be mustered to support that argument?

3. What evidentiary foundation must be presented to have the breathalyzer reading admitted into evidence?

   How would you qualify the breathalyzer operator, Officer Yale?

   How would you establish that Officer Yale followed the proper testing procedures?

   How would you qualify the breathalyzer machine (show it was operating properly and producing accurate readings)?

ASSIGNMENT FOR CLASS

In class, conduct the direct examination of Officer Yale, presenting (a) the foundation for the breathalyzer test, (b) Officer Yale's opinion as to Hard's intoxication, and (c) information contained in the Alcohol Influence Report. Plan to use documentary, demonstrative, and/or real evidence unless your instructor indicates otherwise.

ASSIGNMENT 45: Defense Attorney: Direct Examination of John Gooding
(August 26 and September 3 Incidents)

John Gooding, defendant Ed Hard's friend, is a witness to two separate incidents. Gooding was with Ed Hard on August 26 at the gas station when Bruno allegedly put a knife to Hard's back and threatened him. Gooding was also at the Garage tavern on September 3. This is the time to present John Gooding's direct examination.

PREPARATION

READ: (1) Trial Case File Entries 1-36, 87, 95 (Rules 401-403, 404, 405, 607, 803), 96, 97, 100-103, 111, 112; (2) Chapter 9, *Trial Advocacy* text.

TIPS FOR THIS ASSIGNMENT

1. What objectives do you plan to accomplish during the direct examination of John Gooding?

2. Which factual points supporting your case theory do you wish to present in Gooding's direct examination?

   How will you argue these points in closing argument to the jury?

   Are there problems with Gooding's expected testimony? How will you deal with them?

3. Imagine that you have a strong suspicion that Ed Hard and John Gooding concocted the story about the gas station incident of August 26 to bolster the self-defense claim.

   What ethical considerations and obligations, if any, govern this situation?

ASSIGNMENT FOR CLASS

In class, conduct the direct examination of John Gooding regarding the events of (a) August 26, 20XX, and (b) September 3, 20XX. Use a diagram and photographs to illustrate his testimony. Plan to use documentary, demonstrative, and/or real evidence unless your instructor indicates otherwise.

Civil Case Assignments

ASSIGNMENT 46: Plaintiffs' Attorney: Preparation of Direct Examination *(Deborah Summers)*

Deborah Summers, your client, is an important witness for your case-in-chief. During her direct examination, she can testify concerning the fight between Ed Hard and Bruno Summers on August 20, the telephone threats made by Hard on August 22, the circumstances surrounding the shooting on September 3, and her emotional distress. You want to prepare her for direct examination.

PREPARATION

READ: (1) Trial Case File Entries 1-88, 92-94, 95 (Rules 104, 401-403, 404, 801-803, 901), 96, 98, 100-102, 104, 105, 111, 112, 118; (2) Chapter 9, *Trial Advocacy* text.

TIPS FOR THIS ASSIGNMENT

1. What objectives do you plan to accomplish during your preparation of Deborah Summers for direct examination?

    Which factual points do you wish to review with her that you may argue in closing argument to prove negligence?

2. You wish to prepare Deborah Summers to testify concerning factual information supporting your legal theory. Examine the elements that you must prove as they are stated in the State of Major civil jury instruction on negligence. List those factual points that you wish to prepare Deborah Summers to testify to on direct examination about the element of unreasonable care.

    How could you argue that Ed Hard negligently killed Bruno Summers, based on Deborah Summers's testimony that on August 20 she heard Ed Hard tell Bruno Summers that he would get him (Bruno) the next time?

    How could you argue negligence by Davola and his employees, based on Deborah Summers's testimony regarding the August 20 incident at the Garage tavern?

3. You need to prepare Deborah Summers to be truthful and also to be perceived as credible by the jury. What instructions would you give her about how to communicate to the jury?

    Would you discuss how she should dress for court?

    What else would you tell her about being an effective witness on direct and cross-examination?

4. While you are routinely preparing Deborah, you ask her if she has ever been convicted of a crime. Suppose that Deborah tells you that she was convicted of a juvenile offense. She then tells you that she will not admit that to anyone else because a friend told her that juvenile offenses are sealed and cannot be discovered. Imagine that the case file does not mention her juvenile record.

What ethical concerns do you have?

What other concerns do you have?

What will you tell Deborah Summers about disclosure of her juvenile criminal history?

How does Major Rule of Evidence 609(d) impact disclosure?

ASSIGNMENT FOR CLASS

In class, meet with and prepare Deborah Summers for direct examination. Plan to use documentary, demonstrative, and/or real evidence unless your instructor indicates otherwise.

ASSIGNMENT 47: Attorney for Defendant Davola: Preparation of Direct Examination (*Tom Donaldson*)

Tom Donaldson is one of the defendants in the civil case, and he may testify at trial. He was the bartender at the Garage tavern. He can testify to the circumstances surrounding the August 20 fight between Bruno Summers and Ed Hard and the shooting on September 3. You want to prepare Tom Donaldson for direct and cross-examination.

PREPARATION

READ: (1) Trial Case File Entries 1-88, 92-94, 95 (Rules 401-403, 407, 803), 96, 98, 100-102, 104, 111, 113, 118, 120; (2) Chapter 9, *Trial Advocacy* text.

TIPS FOR THIS ASSIGNMENT

1. Preparation includes direct examination and the likely cross-examination. What are the objectives you want to accomplish in preparing Tom Donaldson for direct examination?

2. You will want to prepare Tom Donaldson to relate to the jury the critical facts supporting the defense theories of the case in an explicit and readily understandable manner.

    List all the defense theories that you will pursue and present on behalf of Donaldson.

3. Suppose that Tom Donaldson tells you, "I am thinking of taking the Fifth Amendment if I testify at trial. I could get into trouble for serving Ed Hard intoxicating beverages."

   What will you say to Tom Donaldson? Why?

   If Donaldson does take the Fifth Amendment, what, if any, sanctions could the trial judge impose?

ASSIGNMENT FOR CLASS

In class, meet with and prepare Tom Donaldson for his direct examination. Plan to use documentary, demonstrative, and/or real evidence unless your instructor indicates otherwise.

ASSIGNMENT 48: Plaintiffs' Attorney: Direct Examination of Deborah Summers

Assume that all your motions in limine have been denied without prejudice. You are ready to proceed with the direct examination of Deborah Summers, your first witness and a key witness.

PREPARATION

READ: (1) Trial Case File Entries; 1-88, 91-94, 95 (Rules 401-403, 404, 601, 602, 609, 613, 801, 803, 901), 96, 98, 101-102, 104-105, 111-113, 118; (2) Chapter 9, *Trial Advocacy* text.

TIPS FOR THIS ASSIGNMENT

1. What are your objectives for the direct examination of Deborah Summers?

2. Think about your order of witnesses. Would you call Deborah Summers as your first or last witness?

3. Now focus on one specific factual point supporting your case theory that you wish Deborah Summers to testify to on direct examination. You would like to have the jury hear all of what Bruno Summers said while Bruno and Deborah were at the Garage on September 3. Suppose that you think part of what Bruno said may be held by the court to be hearsay.

Will you still ask Deborah to relate it to the jury?

What ethical problem, if any, would you face if you present the above testimony?

ASSIGNMENT FOR CLASS

In class, conduct the direct examination of Deborah Summers according to your instructor's specific assignment. Plan to use documentary, demonstrative, and/or real evidence unless your instructor indicates otherwise.

ASSIGNMENT 49: Plaintiffs' Attorney: Direct Examination of Bert Kain

Your next witness for direct examination is Bert Kain. Preceding witnesses whom you have called in your case-in-chief included Deborah Summers and Peter Dean. Except for minor conflicts, the accounts by Summers and Dean were consistent with Deborah Summers's deposition.

Bert Kain is a witness to the two incidents at the Garage tavern on August 20, 20XX, and September 3, 20XX. Police detectives interviewed Kain shortly after the shooting of Bruno Summers on September 3. However, they did not take a statement from him until September 7, 20XX + 1. At that time, Kain told the detectives that although he did not see the shooting on September 3, 20XX, after the shooting he saw Ed Hard standing in the tavern with a gun in his hand. According to Kain, Hard was smiling and said, "Good job."

PREPARATION

READ: (1) Trial Case File Entries 1-88, 92-94, 95 (Rules 401-403, 613), 96, 98, 100-102, 104, 111, 112, 113, 118; (2) Chapter 9, *Trial Advocacy* text.

TIPS FOR THIS ASSIGNMENT

1. What objectives do you wish to accomplish during your direct examination of Bert Kain?

   What testimony by Kain would you discuss in closing argument?

2. What are the main factual points in terms of your case theory that you wish to present in Kain's direct examination?

   Are there problems with Kain's story? How will you deal with these problems?

3. Suppose that Bert Kain complains to you that he will lose a day of work coming to court and he wants your office to pay the difference between the statutory witness fee and his lost wages.

   What ethical concerns, if any, do you have about complying with this request?

ASSIGNMENT FOR CLASS

In class, conduct the direct examination of Bert Kain. Plan to use documentary, demonstrative, and/or real evidence unless your instructor indicates otherwise.

ASSIGNMENT 50: Plaintiffs' Attorney: Direct Examination of Roberta Montbank

Ms. Montbank was an eyewitness to the shooting on September 3, 20XX, at the Garage tavern. The police mistakenly understood her name was Robin Luntlebunk and thus could not find her. But an investigator for EKKO, the insurance company for Davola, the tavern owner, located Ms. Montbank and took her statement on October 26, 20XX. On November 3, 20XX, she gave a written statement to the police; a deposition was taken on May 1, 20XX + 1.

The scale diagram and photographs of the Garage tavern have already been admitted into evidence. Witnesses you have already called to testify are Deborah Summers, Peter Dean, and Bert Kain. Present the testimony of Roberta Montbank.

PREPARATION

READ: (1) Trial Case File Entries 1-88, 92-94, 95 (Rules 401-403, 601, 612, 613, 803), 96, 98, 100-102, 104, 111, 113, 117, 118; (2) Chapter 9, *Trial Advocacy* text.

TIPS FOR THIS ASSIGNMENT

1. What are your objectives for direct examination of Roberta Montbank? A word of caution: Roberta's testimony is as fraught with difficulties as it is important to your case. What are the difficulties?

2. Imagine that during direct examination Ms. Montbank cannot remember where she sat in the Garage tavern on September 3, 20XX. What will you do? Suppose that you show her the signed statement she

gave to the police, and it does not refresh her recollection. What will you do?

Even if Roberta Montbank's statement is read to the jury, how, if at all, can you avoid also giving the jury information that Ms. Montbank has a failing memory and, perhaps, generally poor perceptual abilities?

Should you attempt to avoid giving this information about her failing memory to the jury?

3. What problems do you anticipate Roberta Montbank will face on cross-examination? How do you plan to deal with them?

ASSIGNMENT FOR CLASS

In class, conduct the direct examination of Roberta Montbank. Your instructor may request that you illustrate Roberta Montbank's testimony by using photographs and a diagram of the Garage, which have already been admitted into evidence. Plan to use documentary, demonstrative, and/or real evidence unless your instructor indicates otherwise.

ASSIGNMENT 51: Plaintiffs' Attorney: Direct Examination of Ronnie Summers (Child Witness)

Ronnie Summers is the son of Bruno Summers by a prior marriage. You are ready to proceed with the direct examination of Ronnie Summers, your last witness, and a key witness on assessing damages. Do not forget to use documentary, demonstrative, and/or real evidence whenever it aids Ronnie's communication.

PREPARATION

READ: (1) Trial Case File Entries 1-88, 92-94, 95 (Rules 401-403, 601, 602, 611, 612), 98, 101, 102, 105, 117, 118; (2) Chapter 9, *Trial Advocacy* text.

TIPS FOR THIS ASSIGNMENT

1. What are your objectives for the direct examination of Ronnie Summers? Now focus on one specific factual point supporting your case theory that you want Ronnie Summers to testify to on direct exami-

nation. Would you like to have the jury hear all of what Ronnie Summers can tell you about his, Amanda's, and Deborah's relationships with Bruno? How will you accomplish this?

2. Are there potential evidentiary problems with his testimony? What evidentiary problems (objections) do you anticipate if you ask Ronnie to relate what his life was like before Deborah and Bruno married and how it is now after Bruno's death? Suppose that you assume part of what Ronnie might say may be ruled by the court to be hearsay. Will you still ask Ronnie to relate it to the jury?

   What ethical problem, if any, would you face if you offer the above testimony?

3. You must be prepared to adjust your direct examination to meet witness problems. What problems might Ronnie Summers present because he is a child?

   Think about how you want Ronnie to present himself (dress, language, demeanor). Will you tell him how to act, dress, and so on?

   Suppose that Ronnie Summers is obviously nervous when he enters the courtroom. How will you calm and reassure him?

   Will you examine Ronnie the same way you would an adult witness?

   Assume that Ronnie were to begin crying. What would you do?

ASSIGNMENT FOR CLASS

In class, conduct the direct examination of Ronnie Summers. Plan to use documentary, demonstrative, and/or real evidence unless your instructor indicates otherwise.

ASSIGNMENT 52: Attorney for Defendant Hard: Direct Examination of Ed Hard

Your main witness is, of course, your client, Ed Hard. Direct examination of your client is the most important testimony in your case. You call Hard as the last witness in the defense case after John Gooding and Rebecca Karr have testified.

Assume that all your motions in limine concerning Ed Hard (prior conviction, photographs) have been denied. Now conduct the direct examination of your client.

PREPARATION

READ: (1) Trial Case File Entries 1-88, 92-94, 95 (Rules 401-403, 404, 405, 609, 613), 96, 98, 100-102, 110-112, 118; (2) Chapter 9, *Trial Advocacy* text.

TIPS FOR THIS ASSIGNMENT

1. What objectives do you want to accomplish during direct examination of Ed Hard?

2. Consider specific factual points in support of your case theories that you need to develop in direct examination.

   List the major factual points on the defense of self-defense.

   List the major factual points on one other defense case theory.

3. What weak points exist in Ed Hard's version of what took place? How will you deal with the weak points on direct examination?

   How do you intend to cope with your client's prior inconsistent statements?

ASSIGNMENT FOR CLASS

In class, conduct the direct examination of Ed Hard according to your instructor's specific assignment. Plan to use documentary, demonstrative, and/or real evidence unless your instructor indicates otherwise.

ASSIGNMENT 53: Attorney for Defendant Davola: Direct Examination of Mary Apple

Mary Apple was on duty and working at the Garage tavern on August 20, 20XX, and September 3, 20XX. On September 5, 20XX, two days after the shooting of Bruno Summers, Detective Tharp interviewed Mary Apple by telephone. According to her deposition, she told him that she could not remember if Ed Hard or Bruno Summers was intoxicated on August 20, but she recalled that Ed Hard was loud and obnoxious. She did not see their fight.

As to the night of the shooting, she told Detective Tharp that Ed Hard had slurred speech and was again loud and obnoxious. She also told the police that in her opinion Bruno Summers was not intoxicated, but he did have "fuzzy" speech when she observed him entering the tavern. Mary Apple also stated at her deposition that she might have said on September 3, "Oh my God, I shouldn't have served them."

PREPARATION

READ: (1) Trial Case File Entries 1-88, 92-94, 95 (Rules 401-403, 407, 613), 96, 98, 100, 102, 110, 111, 118; (2) Chapter 9, *Trial Advocacy* text.

TIPS FOR THIS ASSIGNMENT

1. What objectives do you wish to accomplish during your direct examination of Mary Apple?

   In terms of your case theory, what are the main factual points that you want to present in Ms. Apple's direct examination?

2. Suppose that Mary Apple is not a convincing witness. She generally responds to questions by prefacing her answers with expressions such as "I guess," "maybe," and so on. How might you deal with this problem during direct examination?

   Mary Apple also chews gum much of the time. Will you tell her during a pretrial witness interview that she should not chew gum?

   What if you do, but she is chewing gum when she is called into the courtroom to testify. What will you do?

ASSIGNMENT FOR CLASS

In class, conduct the direct examination of Mary Apple. Plan to use documentary, demonstrative, and/or real evidence unless your instructor indicates otherwise.

Chapter 10. Cross-Examination: Concession Seeking

Criminal Case Assignments

ASSIGNMENT 54: Defense Attorney: Cross-Examination of Peter Dean

It is time to cross-examine the prosecutor's second witness, Peter Dean. He was the best man at the wedding of Bruno and Deborah Summers on August 27. He also was present when Bruno Summers received the telephone call Ed Hard allegedly made on August 22, and he accompanied Deborah and Bruno Summers to the Garage tavern on the night of September 3.

Assume that Peter Dean will testify in accordance with his statement in the Case File Entry 72 and that the prosecutor's motion in limine was denied by the judge.

PREPARATION

READ: (1) Trial Case File Entries 1-36, 72, 87, 95 (Rules 401-403, 404, 406, 602, 803, 901), 96, 97, 100, 102, 103; (2) Chapter 10, *Trial Advocacy* text.

TIPS FOR THIS ASSIGNMENT

1. What concessions in support of your case theory do you intend to elicit from Peter Dean through cross-examination?

   How, if at all, do you plan to discredit Peter Dean or his testimony during cross-examination?

2. Think about alternatives to cross-examination that you could use to prevent damaging testimony of Peter Dean. How will you act if the alternative measures are unsuccessful?

   How could you attempt to exclude from evidence what Bruno Summers said after receiving the alleged telephone call from your client on August 22?

   Suppose that the statement by Bruno was admitted as an excited utterance. How would you deal with it on cross-examination?

3. If you had no direct evidence that Peter Dean knew Bruno Summers was carrying a knife on September 3, would you ask, in an effort to obtain a favorable admission, "On September 3, you knew Bruno Summers was carrying a knife, didn't you?"

   Would you ask the witness whether Bruno Summers habitually carried a knife?

   Is there any ethical problem with such a question?

ASSIGNMENT FOR CLASS

In class, conduct the cross-examination of Peter Dean. Plan to use documentary, demonstrative, and/or real evidence unless your instructor indicates otherwise.

ASSIGNMENT 55: Defense Attorney: Cross-Examination of Fred Faye

Mr. Faye is the owner of the American Gun Shop. He allegedly sold the fatal .22-caliber revolver to Ed Hard. Mr. Faye retained the dealer's copies of the Application to Transfer Pistol or Revolver and the Firearms Transaction Record, which bear the written signature, "Edward Taylor Hard." He also has a copy of a canceled check bearing the same signature. Prior to calling Mr. Faye, the prosecutor has called Deborah Summers and Peter Dean as witnesses. During his direct examination, Mr. Faye identifies the defendant as the purchaser of the revolver. Cross-examine Fred Faye.

PREPARATION

READ: (1) Trial Case File Entries 1-36, 87, 95 (Rules 401-403, 801-803, 901, 902, 1001-1004), 96, 97, 101; (2) Chapter 10, *Trial Advocacy* text.

TIPS FOR THIS ASSIGNMENT

1. What concessions supporting your case theory do you plan on eliciting through cross-examination of Fred Faye?

    How could Mr. Faye's testimony prove beneficial to the defense case theory?

2. How, if at all, do you intend to discredit Fred Faye or his testimony during cross-examination?

    How central a witness is Mr. Faye in this case (crucial, cumulative, peripheral)?

    What does this witness contribute to the prosecutor's case theory?

3. Will you attempt to discredit Fred Faye's identification of Ed Hard as the purchaser of the gun?

    Imagine that you know for certain that Mr. Faye is a truthful witness. Do you think any ethical problem exists in using cross-examination to confuse him or make him look indecisive?

ASSIGNMENT FOR CLASS

In class, conduct the cross-examination of Fred Faye. Plan to use documentary, demonstrative, and/or real evidence unless your instructor indicates otherwise.

ASSIGNMENT 56: Defense Attorney: Cross-Examination of Cindy Rigg

Cindy Rigg, who was a patron in the Garage on August 20, observed the fight between Bruno Summers and Edward Hard. Cindy Rigg is the prosecutor's fourth witness; she follows Deborah Summers, Peter Dean, and Fred Faye.

Assume that this witness testified to the information contained in the written statement in Trial Case File Entry 20, unless your instructor informs you otherwise. It is now your opportunity to cross-examine Cindy Rigg.

PREPARATION

READ: (1) Trial Case File Entries 1-36, 87, 94, 95 (Rules 401-403, 404, 801-803), 96, 97, 100, 110; (2) Chapter 10, *Trial Advocacy* text.

TIPS FOR THIS ASSIGNMENT

1. Consider how the cross-examination of Cindy Rigg may be used to obtain admissions supporting your case theory. How central a witness is Cindy Rigg in this case?

   What evidence presented on direct examination of Ms. Rigg would help establish the defense theory of the case?

   What testimony hurts the defense case?

2. Focus your attention on the self-defense theory of the case. How could you use the August 20 fight to support your closing argument on self-defense? According to Cindy Rigg, what were the relative physical builds of Ed Hard and Bruno Summers?

3. Besides obtaining concessions, what other objectives, if any, do you plan on accomplishing during cross-examination of Cindy Rigg?

4. How might your cross-examination discredit the witness or her testimony? Specifically, think about comparing and contrasting Cindy Rigg's testimony with that of other witnesses to expose any weakness in her ability to accurately recount what happened. Would you use the diagram of the Garage tavern during cross-examination to point out why she may have had difficulty seeing and hearing what happened?

   Do Cindy Rigg and Deborah Summers describe the fight in the same manner?

   How might you use conflicts between the testimony of Cindy Rigg and Deborah Summers during closing argument?

ASSIGNMENT FOR CLASS

In class, conduct the cross-examination of Cindy Rigg. Plan to use documentary, demonstrative, and/or real evidence unless your instructor indicates otherwise.

ASSIGNMENT 57: Defense Attorney: Cross-Examination of Officer Yale

Officer Yale arrested the defendant Ed Hard, seized a .22-caliber revolver from his residence, and administered Hard's breathalyzer test. Officer Yale testified on direct examination in a manner consistent with his prior written statement and the Alcohol Influence Report. Witnesses who have already testified include all lay witnesses and Officer West.

PREPARATION

READ: (1) Trial Case File Entries 1-36, 87, 94, 95 (Rules 401-403, 613, 701-705), 99, 100, 110; (2) Chapter 10, *Trial Advocacy* text.

TIPS FOR THIS ASSIGNMENT

1. In general, what objectives do you want to accomplish through your cross-examination of Officer Yale?

   If the prosecutor did not mention the beer bottles Yale observed at Ed Hard's residence, would you bring this information out on cross-examination?

2. Consider the impact of Officer Yale's testimony on a defense theory of intoxication as a defense. Can you use cross-examination as a means of obtaining concessions supporting that theory?

3. Would you make any effort to exclude from evidence either the information contained in the Alcohol Influence Report or the form itself?

   Can you attack the reliability of the breathalyzer test procedures or of the machine itself?

   What can you gain in this case if you are successful?

   Should you attack the breathalyzer test results with the same intensity you would in a drunk driving case?

How would the exclusion of this evidence affect your cross-examination of Officer Yale or your closing argument concerning Officer Yale?

4. Think about attempting to discredit Officer Yale or his testimony through your cross-examination. Are there problems in cross-examining a police officer that are not present in cross-examining civilian witnesses?

How does this affect your approach to Officer Yale?

ASSIGNMENT FOR CLASS

In class, conduct the cross-examination of Officer Yale. Plan to use documentary, demonstrative, and/or real evidence unless your instructor indicates otherwise.

ASSIGNMENT 58: Prosecutor: Cross-Examination of John Gooding

Assume that this witness testified to the information contained in his written statement in Trial Case File Entry 25, unless your instructor informs you otherwise.

John Gooding is a witness to the gas station incident on August 26, 20XX, and to the events in the Garage on August 20 and September 3. He is a character witness for Ed Hard and has also testified to Bruno Summers's reputation for violence. John Gooding is the second witness presented during the defense case.

PREPARATION

READ: (1) Trial Case File Entries 1-36, 87, 95 (Rules 401-403, 404, 405, 607, 701), 96, 97, 100-102, 110 (2) Chapter 10, *Trial Advocacy* text.

TIPS FOR THIS ASSIGNMENT

1. What concessions in support of your case theory do you intend to obtain through cross-examination of John Gooding?

How, if at all, do you plan to discredit John Gooding or his testimony?

2. Think about Gooding's testimony about Ed Hard's good reputation for peacefulness. Would you attack the evidentiary foundation for admissibility of this testimony? If so, how? If not, why?

3. What questions may you properly ask character witness Gooding about Ed Hard's prior conduct?

   What is your legal authority?

   How should you phrase the questions?

   Can you introduce extrinsic evidence concerning Ed Hard as a result of John Gooding's denial of any knowledge of Ed Hard's bad conduct?

   What objections do you expect from opposing counsel? How will you respond?

4. Imagine that you learned from one of Ed Hard's painting customers that money mysteriously disappeared from the house on the day Ed Hard painted it. Would you ask about this?

   Is there an ethical problem in asking, "Have you heard that defendant Hard stole from houses he was painting?"

ASSIGNMENT FOR CLASS

In class, conduct the cross-examination of John Gooding. Plan to use documentary, demonstrative, and/or real evidence unless your instructor indicates otherwise.

ASSIGNMENT 59: Prosecutor: Cross-Examination of Ed Hard

The most crucial cross-examination of the case—that of the defendant, Ed Hard—is next. The success of your case may well rise or fall on the jury's assessment of Ed Hard. He is the last witness in the trial.

Assume that all motions in limine have been denied. Also assume that Hard testified to the information contained in the written statement in Trial Case File Entry 17, unless your instructor informs you otherwise. Now conduct the cross-examination of Ed Hard.

PREPARATION

READ: (1) Trial Case File Entries 1-36, 87, 95 (Rules 401-403, 609, 611, 613), 96, 97, 100-102, 110-112; (2) Chapter 10, *Trial Advocacy* text.

TIPS FOR THIS ASSIGNMENT

1. What concessions in support of your case theory do you intend to elicit through your cross-examination of Ed Hard?

    How, if at all, do you plan to discredit Ed Hard or his testimony?

2. Now consider attempting to gain admissions that would develop Ed Hard's motive for shooting and killing Bruno Summers. How could you do this?

    Can you develop Ed Hard's motive without also making his fear of Bruno Summers seem more reasonable?

    How does motive fit in with your theory of the case?

3   Imagine that Ed Hard testified on direct examination that the handgun discharged accidentally. On cross-examination, how, if at all, would you discredit this portion of Ed Hard's direct examination testimony?

ASSIGNMENT FOR CLASS

In class, conduct the cross-examination of Ed Hard. Plan to use documentary, demonstrative, and/or real evidence unless your instructor indicates otherwise.

Civil Case Assignments

ASSIGNMENT 60: Attorneys for Defendants Hard and Davola: Cross-Examination of Deborah Summers

The first witness to be called by plaintiffs is Deborah Summers, who you anticipate will be a key witness for the plaintiffs.

Assume that the court has denied without prejudice all of plaintiffs' attorney's motions in limine. Also assume that this witness testified to the information contained in the written statement in Trial Case File Entry 21 unless your instructor informs you otherwise. It is now your opportunity to cross-examine Deborah Summers.

PREPARATION

READ: (1) Trial Case File Entries 1-88, 91-94, 95 (Rules 401-403, 404, 609, 613), 96, 98, 100-102, 104, 105, 111, 112, 113, 118; (2) Chapter 10, *Trial Advocacy* text.

TIPS FOR THIS ASSIGNMENT

1. What concessions in support of your case theory do you plan on obtaining during cross-examination of Deborah Summers?

   Are these concessions the same for both defendants Hard and Davola?

   What points are similar?

   What points differ?

2. How, if at all, do you intend to discredit Deborah Summers or her testimony through cross-examination?

3. Suppose that you have obtained Deborah Summers's juvenile court file, which lists the following: truancy (case diverted); a school burglary (convicted and placed on probation); and violation of the Uniform Controlled Substances Act for possession of cocaine (convicted and placed on probation). (See Trial Case File Entry 51.) Plaintiffs' attorney has not made a motion in limine to prohibit you from inquiring about these matters, even though one interpretation of Major Rule of Evidence 609(d) might appear to preclude it.

   Would you cross-examine Deborah Summers about the prior convictions?

   Assume that the court allowed you to cross-examine her about her adjudications and she denied them.

   What would you do? What, if any, ethical problem would exist if you asked her about the record for truancy?

ASSIGNMENT FOR CLASS

Assume the role of attorney for defendant Hard and then the role of attorney for defendant Davola, unless your instructor indicates otherwise. In class, conduct the cross-examination of Deborah Summers according to your instructor's specific assignment. Plan to use documentary, demonstrative, and/or real evidence unless your instructor indicates otherwise.

ASSIGNMENT 61: Attorneys for Defendants Davola and Hard: Cross-Examination of Bert Kain

Bert Kain is a witness to the incidents on August 20, 20XX, and September 3, 20XX, at the Garage tavern.

Bert Kain testified on direct examination that he was at the Garage tavern on August 20 and September 3. Kain was asked primarily about two issues: first, the statement he claims he overheard Mary Apple make, "Oh my God, I shouldn't have served them," and whether this statement was made on August 20 or September 3; second, Kain's description of Ed Hard smiling and saying, "Good job," after the shooting of Bruno Summers. Kain has discussed these two issues inconsistently in his statement to Detective Tharp and in his deposition. During direct examination, however, Kain testified: "I am positive I heard Apple's 'Oh my God' statement on September 3 and I heard Hard say, 'Good job,' and saw his smile."

Before calling Kain as a witness, plaintiffs already called as witnesses Deborah Summers and Peter Dean. Now it is your opportunity to cross-examine Bert Kain. For this assignment, assume that this witness testifies to information as indicated in his statement in the Trial Case File Entry 18 and in the introduction of this assignment, unless your instructor indicates otherwise.

PREPARATION

READ: (1) Trial Case File Entries 1-88, 92-94, 95 (Rules 401-403, 613, 801-803), 96, 98, 102, 111, 118; (2) Chapter 10, *Trial Advocacy* text.

TIPS FOR THIS ASSIGNMENT

1. In general, what objectives do you plan to accomplish during your cross-examination of Bert Kain?

   What concessions supporting your case theory will you seek during cross-examination?

2. Cross-examination is one method of meeting the potential testimony of witnesses. Think about other methods of excluding all or part of Bert Kain's testimony. Would you object to direct testimony by Bert Kain concerning what he claims Mary Apple said on September 3?

   Suppose you did object. What would be the legal basis for the objection?

   How do you anticipate plaintiffs' attorney will respond to the objection?

ASSIGNMENT FOR CLASS

Assume the role of attorney for defendant Davola and then the role of attorney for defendant Hard, unless your instructor indicates otherwise. In class, conduct the cross-examination of Bert Kain. Plan to use documentary, demonstrative, and/or real evidence unless your instructor indicates otherwise.

ASSIGNMENT 62: Attorneys for Defendants Davola and Hard: Cross-Examination of Roberta Montbank

Roberta Montbank was an eyewitness to the shooting on September 3 and is an essential witness for plaintiffs.

Roberta Montbank is plaintiffs' fourth witness, after Deborah Summers, Peter Dean, and Bert Kain. During direct examination, Ms. Montbank had a tendency to give rambling, nonresponsive answers. Although basically she testified as her statement and deposition indicated she would, Ms. Montbank stated during direct examination that she was sitting in the front of the tavern on September 3 and then corrected herself and said she sat in the back of the tavern. She finally said: "That's funny, dearie. Now I'm not sure. I can't remember." Her memory was later refreshed and she then stated: "Oh, that's helpful. Yes, now I remember. I was sitting in the front of the tavern."

When questioned on direct examination, Ms. Montbank said she did not remember telling the police on November 3, 20XX, that she "heard the shorter man . . . say, 'It's about time.'" When shown her statement to refresh her memory, she stated on direct: "I'm sorry, dearie. I just can't remember if Hard said anything before the shooting, even if that paper you just showed me says that I said he did."

It is time to cross-examine Roberta Montbank. Assume that this witness testified to the information contained in the written statement in Trial Case File Entry 19, unless your instructor informs you otherwise.

PREPARATION

READ: (1) Trial Case File Entries 1-88, 92-94, 95 (Rules 401-403, 601, 612, 613, 803), 96, 98, 102, 111, 117, 118; (2) Chapter 10, *Trial Advocacy* text.

TIPS FOR THIS ASSIGNMENT

1. What concessions in support of your case theory do you intend to elicit from Roberta Montbank through cross-examination?

2. How, if at all, do you plan to discredit Roberta Montbank or her testimony?

   Roberta Montbank did not give a statement to the police until November 3. Is there any ethical problem with your attempting to discredit her for the late report, although you know it was a result of innocent inadvertence on her part and that of the police?

3. Ms. Montbank is the type of witness who rambles and is inadvertently evasive. How will you deal with this problem without causing the jury to sympathize with her?

ASSIGNMENT FOR CLASS

Assume the role of attorney for defendant Davola and then the role of attorney for defendant Hard, unless your instructor indicates otherwise. In class, conduct the cross-examination of Roberta Montbank. Plan to use documentary, demonstrative, and/or real evidence unless your instructor indicates otherwise.

ASSIGNMENT 63: Attorney for Defendant Hard: Cross-Examination of Ronnie Summers

The last witness to be called by plaintiffs was Ronnie Summers, who, as you anticipated, proved to be an emotional witness for plaintiffs. On direct examination, Ronnie testified about his relationship with his father Bruno, including the activities they shared, the loss of companionship since his father's death, and so on. Plaintiffs' attorney also used photographs of Christmas 20XX-1 and of the picnic in August 20XX, which are in evidence. It is now your opportunity to cross-examine Ronnie Summers.

PREPARATION

READ: (1) Trial Case File Entries 1-88, 92-94, 95 (Rules 401-403, 601 602, 611, 613), 96, 98, 101, 102, 104, 117, 118; (2) Chapter 10, *Trial Advocacy* text.

TIPS FOR THIS ASSIGNMENT

1. What concessions in support of your case theory do you plan to obtain during cross-examination of Ronnie Summers?

2. How, if at all, do you intend to discredit Ronnie Summers or his testimony through cross-examination?

3. What problems do you anticipate in cross-examining a child, and how will you deal with the problems?

ASSIGNMENT FOR CLASS

In class, conduct the cross-examination of Ronnie Summers. Plan to use documentary, demonstrative, and/or real evidence unless your instructor indicates otherwise.

ASSIGNMENT 64: Plaintiffs' Attorney: Cross-Examination of Mary Apple

Mary Apple was on duty and working at the Garage on August 20, 20XX, and September 3, 20XX. On September 5, 20XX, Detective Tharp interviewed Mary Apple by telephone. At that time, she told the detective that, as to August 20, she could not remember if Ed Hard or Bruno Summers was intoxicated, but she did remember that Ed Hard was loud and obnoxious. She also said that she did see their fight. As to the night of the shooting, September 3, she told Detective Tharp that Ed Hard had slurred speech and was loud and obnoxious. She also told the police that in her opinion Bruno Summers was not intoxicated, but he did have "fuzzy" speech when he entered the tavern.

Mary Apple had her deposition taken on May 23, 20XX + 1. In response to a question by plaintiffs' attorney as to the incidents on September 3, she admitted that she might have said on that night, "Oh my God, I shouldn't have served them." Recall that Bert Kain, a witness for plaintiffs, testified on direct examination that he was at the Garage tavern on August 20, 20XX, and September 3, 20XX. He also testified that on September 3 he was at the back of the tavern and, although he did not actually see the shooting, he heard Mary Apple scream, "Oh my God, I shouldn't have served them."

However, during her direct examination Mary Apple testified, "I think I said, 'Oh my God, I shouldn't have served them,' on August 20th." She also testified that neither Hard nor Summers was intoxicated on either August 20 or September 3. Otherwise, her testimony was consistent with what she told Detective Tharp on September 5, 20XX. When asked during her direct examination why she told the police Hard was intoxicated on the night of September 3, she said, "Well, I guess I was mistaken when I spoke to the police. I was upset."

Mary Apple is the second defense witness for defendant Davola after Tom Donaldson. Donaldson was the bartender at the Garage tavern on August 20 and September 3. Now is your opportunity to cross-examine Mary Apple. For this assignment, assume that the witness testifies as stated in the introduction to the assignment, unless your instructor indicates otherwise.

PREPARATION

READ: (1) Trial Case File Entries 1-88, 92-94, 95 (Rules 401-403, 407, 613, 801-804), 96, 98, 100, 102, 110, 111, 113, 118; (2) Chapter 10, *Trial Advocacy* text.

TIPS FOR THIS ASSIGNMENT

1. What, if any, concessions in support of your case theory do you intend to obtain from Mary Apple through cross-examination?

2. How, if at all, do you plan to discredit Mary Apple or her version of events? Will you use the police report?

   Her deposition? If so, what, if any, objections from defense counsel can you anticipate?

3. Concerning Mary Apple's perception of the events on August 20, your approach is unlike what you adopted for other defense witnesses. You want your cross-examination to focus on what Mary Apple heard and saw. Why?

   What did Mary Apple hear and see?

   How would you discuss Mary Apple's testimony in closing argument?

ASSIGNMENT FOR CLASS

In class, conduct the cross-examination of Mary Apple. Plan to use documentary, demonstrative, and/or real evidence unless your instructor indicates otherwise.

ASSIGNMENT 65: Plaintiffs' Attorney: Cross-Examination of Ed Hard

The most crucial cross-examination of the case is that of the defendant, Ed Hard. The success of your case may well rise or fall on the jury's assessment of Ed Hard. He is the last witness in the trial.

Assume that all motions in limine have been denied. Assume that this witness testified to the information contained in the written statement in

Trial Case File Entry 17, unless your instructor informs you otherwise. Now conduct the cross-examination of Ed Hard.

PREPARATION

READ: (1) Trial Case File Entries 1-88, 92-94, 95 (Rules 401-403, 404, 609, 613), 96, 98, 100-102, 110, 111, 112, 113, 118; (2) Chapter 10, *Trial Advocacy* text.

TIPS FOR THIS ASSIGNMENT

1. What objectives do you plan to accomplish during cross-examination of Ed Hard?

2. Now consider specific factual points in support of your case theory that you need to develop in cross-examination.

3. Think about using your cross-examination to undercut the defense's case theory.

   List the major factual points supporting your attack on the defense of self-defense.

   List the major factual points you would bring out to rebut one other defense case theory.

4. What weak points exist in Ed Hard's version of what took place?

   How will you deal with the weak points on cross-examination?

   How do you intend to cope with Hard's prior inconsistent statements?

ASSIGNMENT FOR CLASS

In class, conduct the cross-examination of Ed Hard. Plan to use documentary, demonstrative, and /or real evidence unless your instructor indicates otherwise.

Chapter 11. Experts: Yours and Theirs

Criminal Case Assignments

ASSIGNMENT 66: Prosecutor: Preparation of an Expert Witness (*Dr. L.R. Jackson, Medical Examiner*)

The expert witness to be prepared is Dr. L.R. Jackson, the chief medical examiner who performed an autopsy on Bruno Summers on September 7, 20XX. Dr. Jackson was assisted during the autopsy by Dr. Dorian Ray Flannery.

PREPARATION

READ: (1) Trial Case File Entries 1-36, 87, 94, 95 (Rules 401-403, 702-705, 803), 96, 99, 110, 111; (2) Chapter 11, *Trial Advocacy* text.

TIPS FOR THIS ASSIGNMENT

1. What objectives do you wish to achieve during the preparation of Dr. L.R. Jackson for direct examination?

   You will need to prepare Dr. Jackson to present his qualifications as an expert during direct examination.

   What specific questions will you ask him about his education and experience in the field of pathology? What exhibits would you consider using during the direct examination of Dr. Jackson?

2. The preparation of an expert witness for direct examination is somewhat different from the preparation of a lay witness. Unless you have a background in the witness's area of expertise, you will need to prepare yourself by learning about the subject matter so your direct examination questions facilitate the effective communication of the expert's qualifications as well as the expert's relevant findings and opinions to the jury. You want to present clear, understandable testimony of fact and opinion by Dr. Jackson. To accomplish this end, you must understand the expert testimony.

   How would you learn about how the autopsy was conducted and the findings and opinion Dr. Jackson can express based on the autopsy?

What questions would you ask Dr. Jackson during witness preparation to clarify matters that are explained neither by the autopsy report nor by the medical glossary (Trial Case File Entry 95)?

3. Will you have Dr. Jackson provide a detailed description of how the autopsy was performed?

   Regarding the fatal wound, describe in your own words where the slug entered and traveled in the body of Bruno Summers. Describe in your own words how the gunshot wound directly caused Bruno Summers's death.

ASSIGNMENT FOR CLASS

In class, meet with and prepare Dr. Jackson for direct examination. Plan to use documentary, demonstrative, and/or real evidence unless your instructor indicates otherwise.

ASSIGNMENT 67: Prosecutor and Defense Attorney: Direct Examination and Cross-Examination of an Expert Witness (H. Tredwell, Firearms Expert)

The prosecutor called as a witness H. Tredwell, a firearms expert. Mr. Tredwell will present expert testimony regarding the following: (1) the operation of the .22-caliber revolver recovered from Ed Hard's residence; (2) the trigger pull for the revolver; (3) the microscope comparison of a test-fired slug with the slug taken from Bruno Summers's body, which disclosed that the slug from Summers's body was fired from the revolver; and (4) the examination and comparison of the hole and the pattern of stippling on Summers's shirt with patterns on pieces of cloth created when Tredwell fired the revolver into them. This proximity testing indicates the distance from the gun barrel to the shirt at time of discharge was not more than three feet.

Exhibits that may be used during Tredwell's direct examination include the following:

1. The .22 caliber revolver—Exhibit #12, which already has been admitted into evidence;

2. One casing and four live rounds removed from the revolver—Exhibit #13, which already has been admitted into evidence;

3. Slug recovered from Bruno Summers's body—Exhibit #7, which already has been admitted into evidence;

4. Bruno Summers's shirt—Exhibit #6, which already has been admitted into evidence;

5. Slug test-fired by Tredwell using the revolver (Exhibit #12)—Exhibit #16, which is premarked but has not been admitted into evidence; and

6. Clothes used in proximity testing—Exhibit #17, which is premarked but has not been admitted into evidence.

All of the prosecution's other witnesses have testified except for Dr. Jackson, the medical examiner, whom the prosecutor intends to call as the final witness after Tredwell testifies.

PREPARATION

READ: (1) Trial Case File Entries 1-36, 87, 94, 95 (Rules 401-403, 702-705, 803, 901), 96, 97, 110, 111, 115; (2) Chapter 11, *Trial Advocacy* text.

TIPS FOR THIS ASSIGNMENT

Assume you are the prosecutor presenting direct examination of Mr. Tredwell.

1. How does Mr. Tredwell's direct testimony assist in establishing your case theory?

   What are the most significant parts of Tredwell's examination? It appears that the identification of Ed Hard as the one who shot Bruno Summers will not be an issue at trial. Why would you bother to offer evidence regarding the firearm comparison?

   How, if at all, does the expert witness's testimony regarding trigger pull fit into your case theory?

   How is Tredwell's testimony important to refuting any of Ed Hard's possible defenses?

2. As prosecutor, you need to plan to qualify Mr. Tredwell as an expert. What foundational requirements must you meet to qualify Tredwell as an expert on firearms comparison?

   In what other fields will Tredwell need to be qualified as an expert in order to elicit all the direct testimony you want?

In order to qualify Tredwell in each of these areas of expertise you have identified, what facts will you seek to elicit during your direct examination to meet the legal foundational requirements?

3. During Mr. Tredwell's direct examination, what demonstrative evidence could you use and why would you use it?

   How would you use demonstrative evidence when Tredwell discusses lands and grooves (markings on the slug)?

Now, assume you are the defense attorney cross-examining Mr. Tredwell.

4. What objectives do you want to accomplish during your cross-examination of Mr. Tredwell?

5. Cross-examination needs to be considered in the context of the entire trial. In the State of Major, the *John Baird* case has been widely reported by the media. In the *Baird* case, a firearms expert testified that a slug taken from a victim's body was fired by a rifle found in John Baird's possession. John Baird was convicted of second degree murder. Later it was determined that Baird's rifle did not fire the slug, and the firearms expert erred in the microscope comparison. Baird was set free after years of confinement. Consider how you could use the *Baird* case in cross-examination and other parts of the trial.

6. Would you ask witness Tredwell about the *Baird* case? Explain how you would phrase the inquiry.

   What objections and grounds do you anticipate from the prosecutor?

7. Assume that Tredwell discovered the error in the *Baird* case and gave a speech to a group of forensic scientists about the case. During the speech, Tredwell stated, "We all are subject to making mistakes as happened in *Baird*. There can be tragic results if we are not cautious in applying our science."

   Would you attempt to use this statement during cross-examination?

   Under what evidentiary rules might it be admissible in evidence?

ASSIGNMENT FOR CLASS

Assume either the role of prosecutor or defense counsel as indicated by your instructor. Prosecutor, be prepared to conduct the direct examination of H. Tredwell. Defense attorney, conduct the cross-examination. Plan to use documentary, demonstrative, and/or real evidence unless your instructor indicates otherwise.

ASSIGNMENT 68: Prosecutor and Defense Attorney: Direct Examination and Cross-Examination of an Expert Witness
(Dr. L.R. Jackson, Medical Examiner)

Chief Medical Examiner L.R. Jackson will be the last witness in the prosecutor's case-in-chief. It is time for the prosecutor to conduct the direct examination and for the defense to conduct the cross-examination of the expert witness, Dr. Jackson.

PREPARATION

READ: (1) Trial Case File Entries 1-36, 87, 94, 95 (Rules 401-403, 702-705, 803), 96, 97, 99, 101, 102, 110, 111, 115; (2) Chapter 11, *Trial Advocacy* text.

TIPS FOR THIS ASSIGNMENT

Assume you are the prosecutor presenting direct examination of Dr. Jackson.

1. What are your objectives for the direct examination of Dr. Jackson?

2. As prosecutor, you want to qualify Dr. Jackson as an expert. What are the prerequisites for presenting a foundation to qualify Dr. Jackson as an expert witness? In what specific fields of expertise do you wish to qualify Dr. Jackson? What would you do if, just as you were beginning to attempt to qualify Dr. Jackson, defense counsel interrupted you by rising, smiling at Dr. Jackson, and stating to the court, "Your honor, the defense will stipulate that Dr. Jackson is an eminently qualified and highly respected expert in pathology. There is no need to delay further. We accept him as an expert in this field."

3. What demonstrative evidence might you as the prosecutor use to illustrate the medical examiner's testimony?

Now assume you are the defense attorney cross-examining Dr. Jackson.

4. During your cross-examination of Dr. Jackson, what objectives do you wish to achieve?

5. Consider Dr. Jackson's testimony and the admissions you may be able to obtain during cross-examination that support the defense theory of the case. What admissions would you highlight on cross-examination and argue during closing argument if your theory of the case is that the state has failed to prove that the gunshot was the proximate cause of death?

   If your defense theory is self-defense?

6. Cross-examination is one method of undercutting a witness's testimony. You need to think about other methods you might use in lieu of, or in conjunction with, your cross-examination. Suppose that the doctor is qualified only as a pathologist and the prosecutor attempts to introduce the findings regarding the blood alcohol analysis done on a sample taken September 3 and to elicit opinions regarding the meaning of the findings.

   What objection and grounds would you state? How might the prosecutor respond to your objection?

   What objection and grounds would you state if the prosecutor tried to introduce the autopsy report during direct examination? Or would you not object?

ASSIGNMENT FOR CLASS

Assume either the role of prosecutor or defense counsel as indicated by your instructor. Prosecutor, be prepared to conduct the direct examination of Dr. L.R. Jackson. Defense attorney, conduct the cross-examination. Plan to use documentary, demonstrative, and/or real evidence unless your instructor indicates otherwise.

Civil Case Assignments

ASSIGNMENT 69: Plaintiffs' Attorney: Preparation of an Expert Witness (*Dr. Brett Day, Treating Physician*)

The expert witness to be prepared is Dr. Brett Day, the medical doctor who treated Bruno Summers at Mercy Hospital from September 3 to the day of his death, September 7.

PREPARATION

READ: (1) Trial Case File Entries 1-88, 92-94, 95 (Rules 401-403, 702-705, 803), 96, 98, 99, 101-103, 110, 112, 115; (2) Chapter 11, *Trial Advocacy* text.

TIPS FOR THIS ASSIGNMENT

1. The preparation of an expert witness for direct examination is somewhat different from the preparation of a lay witness. Unless you have a background in the witness's area of expertise, you will need to prepare yourself by learning about the subject matter so your direct examination questions facilitate the effective communication of the expert's qualifications as well as the expert's relevant findings and opinions to the jury.

    What objectives do you wish to achieve during the preparation of Dr. Brett Day for direct examination?

2. Your theory of the case is that Ed Hard and M.C. Davola and his employees are responsible for the wrongful death of Bruno Summers because Hard negligently shot and killed Bruno Summers.

    What opinion would you prepare Dr. Day to present so that during closing argument you can argue that Dr. Day's opinion proves elements of negligence?

    Regarding the gunshot wound being the proximate cause of Bruno Summers's death, what testimony would you hope Dr. Day would be able to express on direct examination?

3. Under the law as set forth in the civil jury instruction on proximate cause (trial case file entry 98), what must plaintiffs' attorney prove to establish the proximate cause element?

    How do you anticipate the defense might cross-examine Dr. Day on the issue of proximate cause?

    How would you prepare Dr. Day to cover the proximate cause issue during direct examination in order to deal with the potential defense attack?

4. Consider exhibits that may be used during the direct examination of Dr. Day.

    What exhibits would you consider using?

ASSIGNMENT FOR CLASS

In class, meet with and prepare Dr. Day for direct examination. Plan to use documentary, demonstrative, and/or real evidence unless your instructor indicates otherwise.

ASSIGNMENT 70: Plaintiffs' and Defendants' Attorneys: Direct Examination and Cross-Examination of an Expert Witness (*Dr. Brett Day, Treating Physician*)

Dr. Brett Day is the medical doctor who treated Bruno Summers at Mercy Hospital for the gunshot wound. Dr. Day was the first expert witness called by plaintiffs' attorney. Now it is time for plaintiffs' attorney to conduct direct examination and for defendants' attorneys to conduct cross-examination of Dr. Day.

PREPARATION

READ: (1) Trial Case File Entries 1-88, 92-94, 95 (Rules 401-403, 702-705, 803), 96, 98, 99, 101-103, 110, 115, 118; (2) Chapter 11, *Trial Advocacy* text.

TIPS FOR THIS ASSIGNMENT

Assume you are plaintiffs' attorney presenting direct examination by Dr. Day.

1. What are your objectives for the direct examination of Dr. Day?

2. How does Dr. Day's testimony support and/or weaken your case theory?

3. What demonstrative evidence might you employ to illustrate Dr. Day's testimony?

Now assume you are either an attorney for defendant Davola or for defendant Hard presenting the cross-examination of Dr. Day.

4. During your cross-examination of Dr. Day, what objectives do you wish to achieve?

5. Consider Dr. Day's testimony and the concessions you may obtain during cross-examination that support the defense theory of the case. What concessions would you highlight on cross-examination and argue during closing argument?

ASSIGNMENT FOR CLASS

Assume either the role of plaintiffs' attorney or of defense counsel for Davola or Hard, as indicated by your instructor. Plaintiffs' attorney, be prepared to conduct the direct examination of Dr. Brett Day. Defendant's attorney, conduct the cross-examination. Plan to use documentary, demonstrative, and/or real evidence unless your instructor indicates otherwise.

ASSIGNMENT 71: Plaintiffs' and Defendants' Attorneys: Direct Examination and Cross-Examination of an Expert Witness (*Dr. Bruce Hann, Economist*)

Economist Dr. Bruce Hann will present expert testimony on plaintiffs' damages. He will be qualified and will give testimony on economic loss. Qualification involves both meeting an evidentiary foundation for admission of his testimony and the presentation of Dr. Hann as a competent, believable expert to the jury.

Dr. Bruce Hann is plaintiffs' attorney's last and most important expert witness on direct examination. Demonstrative evidence may be used in explaining his expert testimony.

Following direct examination by plaintiffs' attorney, attorneys for defendants Davola and Hard will conduct cross-examination.

PREPARATION

READ: (1) Trial Case File Entries 1-88, 92-94, 95 (Rules 401-403, 702-705, 803), 96, 98, 101, 102, 110, 115, 118; (2) Chapter 11, *Trial Advocacy* text.

TIPS FOR THIS ASSIGNMENT

Assume you are plaintiffs' attorney presenting the direct examination of Dr. Hann.

1. How do you plan to use Dr. Hann's direct testimony to establish your case theory? What are the most significant parts of Dr. Hann's examination?

It appears at this juncture that most of the background information about Bruno Summers will not be an issue. Would you bother to present testimony on specific periods in Bruno Summers's life that Dr. Hann relied on?

2. As plaintiffs' attorney, think about how your presentation of Dr. Hann's specific calculations can be used to enrich the communication of your case theory to the jury. How you and Dr. Hann present these calculations and background information during the trial is important.

   Are there any problems in presenting the underlying data that Dr. Hann used for calculating economic loss?

   How would you deal with the potential problems concerning the statistical data?

   How would you deal with a potential problem concerning the factual data?

   Presenting Dr. Hann's specific calculations might be quite technical and difficult to understand because of the mathematics involved. List all the ways you could deal with this potential problem.

   Think about presenting the specific mathematical calculations. Would this be advantageous or would it create problems?

3. What demonstrative evidence might you use during Dr. Hann's direct examination?

Now assume you are either an attorney for defendant Davola or for defendant Hard conducting the cross-examination of Dr. Hann.

4. What objectives do you want to accomplish during your cross-examination of Dr. Hann?

5. As Davola's or Hard's defense attorney, think about the entire trial and the interplay between the testimony of different witnesses. Is there an area of Dr. Hann's direct testimony that you could use to corroborate a defense theory?

   Imagine that Ronnie Summers on cross-examination testified that when his father, Bruno Summers, spent time with him on weekends, his father was usually drinking beer or wine. How might you use Ronnie's testimony in closing argument regarding Dr. Hann's opinion as to economic loss? How could you highlight the conflict between Dr. Hann's finding and opinion, and Ronnie Summers's version of loss of companionship and service?

ASSIGNMENT FOR CLASS

Assume either the role of plaintiffs' attorney or of defendant Davola's or Hard's attorney, as indicated by your instructor. Plaintiffs' attorney, be prepared to conduct the direct examination of Dr. Bruce Hann. Defendant's attorney, conduct cross-examination. Plan to use documentary, demonstrative, and/or real evidence unless your instructor indicates otherwise.

ASSIGNMENT 72: Defendants' and Plaintiffs' Attorneys: Direct Examination and Cross-Examination of an Expert Witness (*Dr. Thomas Monday, Economist*)

Dr. Thomas Monday is defendant's economic expert. He is the first expert witness called by the defendants' attorneys. The defense wants to present expert testimony to minimize the economic loss related to the death of Bruno Summers.

Although defendants' attorneys have cross-examined plaintiffs' economist, Dr. Bruce Hann, presenting their own economist will give the jury an opportunity to compare economic loss figures, which, if liability is found, may significantly lessen the jury's award of damages—or so the defense hopes.

PREPARATION

READ: (1) Trial Case File Entries 1-88, 92-94, 95 (Rules 401-403, 702-705, 803), 96, 98, 101, 102, 110, 115, 118; (2) Chapter 11, *Trial Advocacy* text.

TIPS FOR THIS ASSIGNMENT

Assume you are either an attorney for defendant Davola or for defendant Hard presenting the direct examination of Dr. Monday.

1. How do you plan to use Dr. Monday's direct testimony to establish your case theory?

   What are the most significant parts of Dr. Monday's examination?

   How, if at all, does Bruno Summers's membership in a neo-Nazi survivalist group fit into Dr. Monday's testimony and defendant Hard's case theory?

2. Suppose as defendant Hard's or defendant Davola's attorney, you have interviewed Dr. Monday and read the reports of both Dr. Hann and Dr. Monday, but you still have only minimal knowledge about economics. Think about what you need to learn and how you would gain the necessary knowledge to effectively present Dr. Monday's direct examination. Consider possible sources of information.

   Is Dr. Monday your best source of information?

   Would you go to the library?

   Which specific sources would you use?

   What benefits would you derive from personally looking at other economic loss reports in advance of trial?

3. Do you need merely to understand the calculations that Dr. Monday did, or are there other areas of Dr. Monday's expertise you need to grasp?

   What demonstrative evidence might you use during Dr. Monday's direct examination?

Now assume you are plaintiffs' attorney conducting the cross-examination of Dr. Monday.

4. What objectives do you wish to accomplish during your cross-examination of Dr. Monday?

5. As plaintiffs' attorney, think about the entire trial and the interplay between the testimony of different witnesses. Is there an area of Dr. Monday's direct testimony that you could use to corroborate plaintiffs' theory?

6. Imagine that Rebecca Karr testified Bruno Summers was a member of a neo-Nazi survivalist group at the time of the shooting. How will you deal with Monday's testimony and Rebecca Karr's testimony in closing argument?

   How could you highlight the conflict between Dr. Hann's and Dr. Monday's findings and opinions based on their versions of Bruno Summers's life expectancy?

ASSIGNMENT FOR CLASS

Assume either the role of defendant Davola's attorney or plaintiffs' attorney as indicated by your instructor. Defendant's attorney, be prepared to conduct the direct examination of Dr. Thomas Monday. Plaintiffs' attorney, conduct cross-examination. Plan to use documentary, demonstrative, and/or real evidence unless your instructor indicates otherwise.

ASSIGNMENT 73: Attorneys for Defendant Davola and Plaintiffs: Direct Examination and Cross-Examination of an Expert Witness (*Dr. Dale Thompson, Hospitality Expert*)

The attorney for defendant Davola intends to call Dr. Dale Thompson, who is an expert in the hospitality industry (restaurant and tavern management). Dr. Thompson can describe his findings regarding the management of the Garage tavern and to express his opinion that it fell within the industry standard of reasonable care to protect its patrons. Now it is time for defendant Davola's attorney to conduct direct examination of Dr. Thompson and for plaintiffs' counsel to cross-examine Dr. Thompson.

PREPARATION

READ: (1) Trial Case File Entries 1-88, 92-94, 95 (Rules 401-403, 702-705, 803), 96, 98, 101, 102, 110, 115, 118; (2) Chapter 11, *Trial Advocacy* text.

TIPS FOR THIS ASSIGNMENT

Assume you are the attorney for defendant Davola presenting the direct examination of Dr. Thompson.

1. What are your objectives for the direct examination of Dr. Thompson?

2. Think about how Dr. Thompson's testimony supports or weakens your case theory regarding negligence.

   What is your legal theory for the admissibility of Dr. Thompson's opinion?

   What are the specific factual points that you must establish through Dr. Thompson's direct testimony in order to support your legal theory?

3. Now assume you are plaintiffs' attorney conducting cross-examination. What objectives do you want to accomplish through cross-examination of Dr. Thompson?

What admissions supporting your case theory would you plan to elicit through your cross-examination of Dr. Thompson?

How, if at all, do you intend to discredit Dr. Thompson or his testimony during cross-examination?

ASSIGNMENT FOR CLASS

Assume the role of defendant Davola's attorney or plaintiffs' attorney as indicated by your instructor. Attorney for defendant Davola, be prepared to conduct the direct examination of Dr. Thompson. Plaintiffs' attorney, conduct cross-examination. Plan to use documentary, demonstrative, and/or real evidence unless your instructor indicates otherwise.

ASSIGNMENT 74: Attorneys for Defendant Hard and Plaintiffs: Direct Examination and Cross-Examination of an Expert Witness (*Dr. Sherman Croup, Medical Doctor*)

Dr. Sherman Croup is a doctor at the Neva County Medical Services Clinic, who saw Deborah Summers concerning her emotional problems. He is defendant Hard's final witness in his case-in-chief. Now it is time for defendant Hard's attorney to conduct the direct examination and for plaintiffs' attorney to conduct the cross-examination of this expert witness.

PREPARATION

READ: (1) Trial Case File Entries 1-88, 92-94, 95 (Rules 401-403, 702-705, 803), 96, 98, 99, 101, 102, 110, 115, 118; (2) Chapter 11, *Trial Advocacy* text.

TIPS FOR THIS ASSIGNMENT

Assume you are the attorney for defendant Hard presenting the direct examination of Dr. Croup.

1. What are your objectives for the direct examination of Dr. Croup?

2. Think about how Dr. Croup's testimony supports or weakens your case theory regarding Deborah Summers's emotional distress. Specifically, consider the jury instruction on emotional distress (trial case file entry 98).

How would you address this part of the instruction: "The Plaintiff's mental distress must be the reaction of a normally constituted reasonable person"?

What do you anticipate plaintiffs' attorney will ask on cross-examination on the issue of "normally constituted reasonable person"?

How will you argue this "normally constituted reasonable person" issue in closing argument?

Regarding the emotional distress, consider these specific questions: How might you use Dr. Croup's testimony concerning Deborah Summers's emotional distress during other parts of the trial, such as jury selection, opening statement, and closing argument?

Suppose Deborah Summers's theory is that as a result of witnessing the shooting, she suffered severe emotional distress. Could you use Dr. Croup's testimony during trial to support a defense response to this contention?

3. As defendant's attorney, in planning Dr. Croup's direct examination, you must speculate about potential cross-examination. Consider how plaintiffs' attorney will attempt to discredit the validity of Dr. Croup's expertise and testimony. How do you anticipate plaintiffs' attorney may cross-examine Dr. Croup concerning his expertise (training, education)?

What specific points in Dr. Croup's testimony are vulnerable to plaintiffs' attack? How might you be able to ward off the "sting" of cross-examination during your direct examination?

Now assume you are plaintiffs' attorney conducting the cross-examination of Dr. Croup.

4. During your cross-examination of Dr. Croup, what objectives do you want to achieve?

5. As plaintiffs' attorney, consider Dr. Croup's testimony and the concessions you may obtain during cross-examination that support Deborah Summers's theory of the case. What admissions would you highlight on cross-examination and argue during closing argument if your theory of the case is that the shooting and killing of Bruno Summers was an act that would cause any young bride of ten days severe emotional distress?

ASSIGNMENT FOR CLASS

Assume the role of defendant Hard's attorney or plaintiffs' attorney as indicated by your instructor. Attorney for defendant Hard, be prepared to conduct the direct examination of Dr. Sherman Croup. Plaintiffs' attorney, conduct the cross-examination. Plan to use documentary, demonstrative, and/or real evidence unless your instructor indicates otherwise.

Chapter 12. Jury Instructions: The Jury's Law

Criminal Case Assignments

ASSIGNMENT 75: Prosecutor: Preparation of Jury Instructions

You consulted relevant pattern instructions as you developed your case theory and tentatively planned your closing argument. Now you should prepare the instructions you will propose to the court in advance of trial. A good way to do this is to review your tentative closing argument, as well as the witnesses and exhibits you will present.

PREPARATION

READ: (1) Trial Case File Entries 1-36, 91, 94-97, 107; (2) Chapter 12, *Trial Advocacy* text.

TIPS FOR THIS ASSIGNMENT

1. What role will your instructions play in the trial?

2. How will your jury instructions affect your witness examinations?

3. Suppose that expert witness Dr. Jackson, the medical examiner, will testify about the Bruno Summers autopsy and cause of death. How can the expert witness instruction help you prepare his testimony?

4. Do you plan to use jury instructions during trial?

    How might you use the instruction on the use of prior convictions in response to a defense motion in limine or objection to the admissibility of Ed Hard's prior conviction?

Which jury instructions might you use to make points during your closing argument?

Will you use any visuals when you discuss specific jury instructions?

5. Many jurisdictions, including the State of Major, have pattern jury instructions.

List the pattern instructions that you want.

Which, if any, pattern (or other) instructions do you tentatively plan to use in your closing argument?

ASSIGNMENT FOR CLASS

1. Your instructor may give you specific directions for this assignment.

Outside of class: (a) Prepare a set of proposed jury instructions. Each instruction should be on a separate page and annotated either with State of Major citations or other legal authority. (b) Hand in a copy of your instructions to your instructor and provide a copy to opposing counsel.

2. In class: Be prepared to discuss your jury instructions.

ASSIGNMENT 76: Defense Attorney: Preparation of Jury Instructions

You consulted relevant pattern instructions as you developed your case theory and tentatively planned your closing argument. Now you should prepare the instructions you will propose to the court in advance of trial. A good way to do this is to review your tentative closing argument, as well as the witnesses and exhibits you will present.

Meanwhile, you must also determine which instructions you will request.

PREPARATION

READ: (1) Trial Case File Entries 1-36, 91, 94-97, 107; (2) Chapter 12, *Trial Advocacy* text.

TIPS FOR THIS ASSIGNMENT

1. What role will your instructions play in the trial?

Which jury instructions might you use to make points during your closing argument?

Will you use any visuals when you discuss specific jury instructions?

2. How will your jury instructions affect your witness examinations?

Regarding specific prior acts of misconduct by Bruno Summers, how could you use the self-defense instruction to argue that his conduct should be admitted into evidence?

3. Suppose that you plan to call Ed Hard as a witness and expect that his prior conviction will be admissible. What jury selection questions might you ask prospective jurors that would rely on the law as stated in the pattern instruction concerning the use of prior convictions?

What do you plan to say in closing argument about the court's instruction on prior convictions?

4. Many jurisdictions, including the State of Major, have pattern jury instructions. List the pattern instructions that you want.

Which, if any, pattern instructions do you tentatively plan to use in your closing argument?

ASSIGNMENT FOR CLASS

1. Your instructor may give you specific directions for this assignment. Outside of class: (a) Prepare a set of proposed jury instructions. Each instruction should be on a separate page and annotated either with State of Major citations or other legal authority. (b) Hand in a copy of your instructions to your instructor and provide a copy to opposing counsel.

2. In class: Be prepared to discuss your jury instructions.

ASSIGNMENT 77: Prosecutor and Defense Attorney: Arguing Jury Instructions

You submitted your proposed jury instructions to the court on the first day of trial. Your proposed instructions cover the degrees of homicide (first and second degree murder, voluntary and involuntary manslaughter). (The instructions you proposed are the pattern jury instructions contained in the trial case file entries 96 and 97, as well as a nonpattern instruction on premeditation.)

At the conclusion of all testimony, the court delivered to you and defense counsel the court's proposed instructions. The court's instructions include the pattern instructions but differ in these respects from the instructions you and opposing counsel proposed. Specifically:

- The court has omitted from its proposed set of instructions the pattern instruction you submitted on self-defense by an aggressor (Instruction 17, Case File Entry 97) and the pattern instruction you submitted on premeditation (Instruction 4, Case File Entry 97).
- The court has included your nonpattern instruction on premeditation as well as a defense nonpattern instruction detailing the bases for assessing "reasonableness" in a self-defense claim.

These two court-adopted instructions are as follows:

COURT INSTRUCTION 1: PREMEDITATION

Premeditated means thought over beforehand. When a person, after any deliberation, forms an intent to take human life, the killing may follow immediately after the formation of the settled purpose and it will still be premeditated. Premeditation must involve more than a moment in time. The law requires some time, however long or short, in which a design to kill is deliberately formed.

COURT INSTRUCTION 2: "REASONABLENESS" IN SELF-DEFENSE

In judging the defendant's actions, you should attempt to place yourself, as a reasonable person, in his position at the time of the incident. You should therefore consider his past and present knowledge, his beliefs, the relative size and strength of the participants, and all other factors bearing on the reasonableness of his actions and his apprehensions under the circumstances at the time, as they appeared to him.

You now must plan to make appropriate arguments against those instructions you oppose, and in favor of those you wish given to the jury.

PREPARATION

READ: (1) Trial Case File Entries 1-36, 91, 94-97, 107; (2) Chapter 12, *Trial Advocacy* text.

TIPS FOR THIS ASSIGNMENT

1. Consider whether your case theory has been hurt by the court's addition of the defense instruction on reasonableness in self-defense to the pattern instruction on self-defense that you submitted (Instruction 16, Case File Entry 93). What is the difference between your proposed instruction and the court's proposed instruction in the area of self-defense?

   Why would the defense favor the addition of the instruction on reasonableness?

   How will the prosecutor argue that the court should not give this instruction?

2. On the premeditation issue, consider (a) how your nonpattern instruction differs from your proposed pattern instruction, which the court rejected; (b) why the defense would prefer making closing argument based on the pattern instruction; and (c) why the prosecutor would rather make closing argument based on your instruction on premeditation, which the court has included in its instructions.

3. A strategic approach is to hold back on an instruction revealing your strategy so that you don't signal your strategic approach to the other side. Does this present any ethical concern in the State of Major?

ASSIGNMENT FOR CLASS

In class, both prosecutor and defense attorney conduct arguments on instructions on the record in open court, according to your instructor's assignment. Assume that it is customary for the court to ask first for the prosecutor's exceptions to instructions.

Civil Case Assignments

ASSIGNMENT 78: Plaintiffs' Attorney: Preparation of Jury Instructions and Verdict Forms; Arguing Instructions

You consulted relevant pattern instructions as you developed your case theory and tentatively planned your closing argument. Now you should prepare the instructions you will propose to the court before trial. A good way to do this is to review your tentative closing argument, the witnesses you will propose, and the evidence you wish to present.

PREPARATION

READ: (1) Trial Case File Entries 1-88, 92-96, 98, 118; (2) Chapter 12, *Trial Advocacy* text.

TIPS FOR THIS ASSIGNMENT

1. What role will your instructions play in the *Summers v. Hard* trial?

2. How will your jury instructions affect your witness examinations?

    Suppose that Ronnie Summers will be testifying on damages.

    How can the damage jury instruction help you prepare his testimony?

3. Do you plan to use jury instructions during trial?

    During which parts of the trial?

    Specifically, which ones might you use to illustrate testimony during closing argument?

    Will you use any visual aids when you discuss specific jury instructions?

4. Many jurisdictions, including the State of Major, have pattern jury instructions. List the pattern instructions that you want.

    Certain instructions are key to a jury's understanding of a case. Which jury instructions are the key instructions in plaintiffs' case? Why?

ASSIGNMENT FOR CLASS

1. Your instructor may give you specific directions for this assignment. Outside of class: (a) Prepare a set of proposed jury instructions. Each instruction should be on a separate page and annotated either with State of Major citations or other legal authority. (b) Hand in a copy of your instructions to your instructor and provide a copy to opposing counsel.

2. In class: Be prepared to discuss your jury instructions. Now argue your jury instructions.

ASSIGNMENT 79: Attorneys for Defendants Hard and Davola: Preparation of Jury Instructions and Verdict Forms; Arguing Instructions

You consulted relevant instructions as you developed your case theory and tentatively planned your closing argument. Now you should begin to prepare and finalize the instructions you will propose to the court before trial. A good way to do this is to review your tentative closing argument, the witnesses you will propose, and the evidence you wish to present. In this way, you can, as you go through the trial, make sure that you have included all necessary and relevant instructions.

PREPARATION

READ: (1) Trial Case File Entries 1-88, 92-96, 98, 112, 118; (2) Chapter 12, *Trial Advocacy* text.

TIPS FOR THIS ASSIGNMENT

Assume the role of defendant Davola's or Hard's attorney as indicated by your instructor.

1. What role will your instructions play in trial? Do you plan to use jury instructions in your closing argument?

    Would you include an instruction on comparative fault? Why or why not?

2. How will your jury instructions affect your witness examinations?

    Suppose that plaintiffs are successful in admitting into evidence all of defendant Hard's prior criminal convictions. What instructions, if any, would you like the judge to give?

    What arguments will plaintiffs make opposing your requests? How will you counter plaintiffs' arguments?

3. Plaintiffs' negligence theory for wrongful death claims that defendant Davola owed a duty to protect Bruno Summers from harm that was, or should have been, foreseeable. Plaintiffs' claim that Ed Hard's shooting of Bruno Summers in the Garage tavern was foreseeable to Davola and to Mary Apple and Tom Donaldson, employees of the tavern. Suppose there is no pattern instruction on foreseeability:

    If you were Davola's attorney, would you draft a foreseeability instruction?

Supposing you will draft a foreseeability instruction, what will be its content? What do you expect will be the response of plaintiffs' attorney? Your reply?

4. Plaintiffs are also relying on negligence per se as a legal theory for wrongful death. Are there any statutes that you believe should or should not be incorporated into the jury instructions? If so, how will you accomplish this (paraphrase, quote, omit)?

ASSIGNMENT FOR CLASS

1. Assume the role either of attorney for defendant Davola or attorney for defendant Hard, according to your instructor's directions. Your instructor may give you specific directions for this assignment. Outside of class: (a) Prepare a set of proposed jury instructions. Each instruction should be on a separate page and annotated either with State of Major citations or other legal authority. (b) Hand in a copy of your instructions to your instructor and provide a copy to opposing counsel.

2. In class: Be prepared to discuss your jury instructions. Now, argue your jury instructions.

Chapter 13. Closing Argument: Art of Argument

Criminal Case Assignments

ASSIGNMENT 80: Prosecutor: Closing Argument

You have come full circle. You began the analysis of your case by structuring the factual and legal aspects of your closing argument for your prima facie case.

At this stage, your final planning involves reviewing all aspects of your presentation in relationship to your case theory and covering the weaknesses in the defense case theories. Suppose that the thrust of the defense cross-examination and the defense case has been two-pronged: self-defense and accident (excusable homicide). Assume also that the court will give the jury instructions on all lesser offenses of homicide.

Now both you and defense counsel have presented your cases, and it is time for you to deliver your closing argument.

PREPARATION

READ: (1) Trial Case File Entries 1-36, 46, 87, 94-97, 99, 100-105, 110-112; (2) Chapter 13, *Trial Advocacy* text.

TIPS FOR THIS ASSIGNMENT

1. Write an outline of your initial closing argument.

    Specifically, what is the central theme for your closing argument?

    How will you present your case theory in human terms that are readily understandable by the jury?

2. To present your case theory, you want to review the elements of the crimes (the law) with the jury and apply the elements to the facts. Would a visual help you in doing this? How would you use it?

    How will you apply the law (elements) of first degree murder to the facts?

    Specifically, what testimony would you refer to in discussing premeditation?

3. Imagine that you believe Ed Hard and John Gooding conspired together to invent the August 26 gas station incident and that you successfully exposed this fabrication during your cross-examination of these two defense witnesses. What, if any, ethical and legal concerns would you have about arguing the following statements? "The defendant and John Gooding concocted the story about the gas station incident. They are both liars."

4. What will be your concluding remarks to the jury as you finish your initial closing argument?

    What ethical or other concerns might you have with the following concluding remarks? "When Deborah Summers saw her husband shot and lying on the floor of the Garage tavern, she believed the defendant had murdered him in cold blood, and she screamed. We have now heard all the evidence and the law. We too believe as she did."

5. You should plan on saving strong responsive points for your rebuttal argument. What major points do you wish to assert in rebuttal?

    What points would you deliver in rebuttal argument if the defense argument focused on self-defense?

What rebuttal argument would you make if the thrust of the defense argument was accident, that is, excusable homicide?

ASSIGNMENT FOR CLASS

In class, deliver your closing argument. Plan to use documentary, demonstrative, and/or real evidence unless your instructor indicates otherwise.

ASSIGNMENT 81: Defense Attorney: Closing Argument

You have come full circle. You began the analysis of your case by structuring the factual and legal aspects of your closing argument for your defense.

At this stage, your final planning involves reviewing all aspects of your presentation in relationship to your case theories and covering the weaknesses in the prosecutor's case theories. During the trial, you have focused on two interrelated defense theories during cross-examination and your case-in-chief: self-defense and excusable homicide (accident). In addition, assume that the court will give the jury instructions on all lesser offenses. The prosecutor's initial closing argument centered on explaining first degree murder, but the prosecutor also argued that at a minimum the defendant committed second degree murder. The prosecutor did not discuss the meaning of reasonable doubt.

Now both parties have presented their respective cases, and it is time for you to deliver your closing argument.

PREPARATION

READ: (1) Trial Case File Entries 1-36, 36, 46, 87, 99-105, 110-112; (2) Chapter 13, *Trial Advocacy* text.

TIPS FOR THIS ASSIGNMENT

1. Consider the overall structure and content of your argument. Would you begin by discussing any points made by the prosecutor?

    How will you argue reasonable doubt?

    If you wish to present a narrow set of issues, which would you choose?

    Would you present all possible defense theories to the jury?

2. Are any of the possible defense theories in conflict with one another? Imagine that you also wish to raise the defense of intoxication. Does the intoxication defense conflict in any way with the self-defense theory?

   Self-defense is a complete defense to all forms of homicide. Suppose you wish to argue self-defense and at the same time argue that the lesser-included crime of involuntary manslaughter was at most what the defendant committed. That is, Hard, with a mental state of criminal negligence, discharged the firearm, killing Summers. How, if at all, would you deal with the conflict during your argument?

3. What ethical or other problems would you have with arguing as follows? "The defendant's freedom and indeed the rest of his life depend on your verdict."

4. What will be your concluding remarks to the jury?

ASSIGNMENT FOR CLASS

In class, deliver your closing argument without any restrictions on what defense theory or theories you wish to choose. Plan to use documentary, demonstrative, and/or real evidence unless your instructor indicates otherwise.

Civil Case Assignments

ASSIGNMENT 82: Plaintiffs' Attorney: Closing Argument

You have come full circle. You began the analysis of your case by structuring the factual and legal aspects of your closing argument for your prima facie case. Now both plaintiffs and defense have presented their respective cases, and it is time for you to deliver your closing argument.

At this stage, your final planning involves reviewing all aspects of your presentation in relationship to your case theory, and distinguishing and discussing the weaknesses in the defense case theories. Suppose the thrust of the Hard defense cross-examination and defense case has been two-pronged: Ed Hard's self-defense and Bruno Summers's contributory negligence. At the same time, Davola's defense has also been two-pronged: lack of foreseeability of violence and Bruno Summers's contributory negligence. Assume also that the court will give jury instructions on all plaintiff and defense theories.

PREPARATION

READ: (1) Trial Case File Entries 1-88, 92-96, 98, 99-105, 111, 112-114, 118; (2) Chapter 13, *Trial Advocacy* text.

TIPS FOR THIS ASSIGNMENT

1. To present your case theory, you want to review the elements of negligence with the jury and apply the elements to the facts.

   Would trial visuals help you? How would you use visuals?

   How will you apply the law (elements) of negligence to the facts?

   Explaining damages is an important aspect of plaintiffs' case. Specifically, what testimony will you refer to in discussing damages?

2. Regarding the contributory negligence defense of Hard and Davola, plan what you will discuss with the jury.

   List the factual points supporting your argument that Bruno Summers was not at fault.

   How would you discuss the relationship between self-defense and the contributory negligence defense?

3. What are the advocacy techniques you will use during closing argument?

   Specifically, what is a central theme for your closing argument?

   How will you present your case theory in human terms that are readily understandable by the jury?

4. What will be your concluding remarks to the jury as you finish your initial closing argument?

5. You should plan on saving strong responsive points for your rebuttal argument. What major points do you wish to assert in rebuttal?

   What rebuttal argument would you deliver if the defense argument focused on self-defense?

   What rebuttal argument would you make if the thrust of the defense argument was contributory negligence?

6. What ethical or other concerns might you have with these concluding remarks? "When Deborah Summers saw her husband shot and lying on the floor of the Garage tavern, she believed the defendants had

killed him in cold blood, and she screamed. We have now heard all the evidence and the law. We too believe as she did."

ASSIGNMENT FOR CLASS

In class, deliver your closing argument. Plan to use documentary, demonstrative, and/or real evidence unless your instructor indicates otherwise.

ASSIGNMENT 83: Attorney for Defendants Hard and Davola: Closing Argument

You have come full circle. You began the analysis of your case by structuring the factual and legal aspects of your closing argument for your defense. Now both sides have presented their respective cases, and it is time to deliver closing arguments.

Your final planning involves reviewing all aspects of your presentation in relationship to your case theories and discussing the weaknesses in the plaintiffs' case theories. During the trial, Ed Hard's counsel has focused on two defense theories during cross-examination and the case-in-chief: Ed Hard's self-defense and Bruno Summers's contributory negligence. Davola's defense has also been two-pronged: lack of foreseeability of violence and Bruno Summers's contributory negligence. In addition, assume that the court will give jury instructions regarding all of plaintiffs' and defendants' theories. Plaintiffs' initial closing argument centered on negligence, negligence per se, emotional distress, and damages. Plaintiffs' attorney also argued that neither defendant's defense was credible in light of the evidence and defense witnesses.

PREPARATION

READ: (1) Trial Case File Entries 1-88, 92-96, 98-105, 111, 112-114, 118; (2) Chapter 13, *Trial Advocacy* text.

TIPS FOR THIS ASSIGNMENT

Assume the role of defendant Davola's or Hard's attorney as indicated by your instructor.

1. What point-making, attention-getting introductory remarks will you make to the jury in your closing argument?

What will be your concluding remarks to the jury?

2. Consider the overall structure and content of your argument. Will you begin by discussing any points made by plaintiffs' attorney?

    If you wish to present a narrow set of issues, which would you choose?

    Would you present all possible defense theories to the jury?

    Are any of your client's possible defense theories in conflict with one another? What conflicts exist between the two defendants' theories?

    Does the contributory negligence defense conflict in any way with Ed Hard's self-defense theory?

    If there is a conflict between the contributory negligence theory and Ed Hard's self-defense theory, how will you discuss it with the jury?

3. As attorney for defendant Hard, focus on your argument on self-defense. What will you say about the law as stated in the self-defense jury instruction?

    What factual points will you present as the basis for your argument that Ed Hard was not an aggressor who under law was precluded from acting in self-defense? How will you explain the law on self-defense to the jury?

    What are the facts you will marshal to argue Ed Hard acted in self-defense?

    Would Bruno Summers's neo-Nazi activities be included in your argument?

    Of what relevance to the self-defense theory is the gas station incident on August 26?

4. Attorney for defendant Davola, focus on your case theories and explain which you will stress in closing argument:

    Intervening cause?

    Lack of proximate cause?

    Contributory negligence by Bruno?

    No duty (foreseeability)?

5. Would you argue damages? Why would you? When in your argument would you argue damages?

    What, if anything, would you say about Bruno Summers's pain and suffering?

ASSIGNMENT FOR CLASS

Assume the role either of attorney for defendant Davola or attorney for defendant Hard, unless your instructor directs otherwise. In class, deliver your closing argument without any restrictions on what defense theory or theories you wish to choose. Plan to use documentary, demonstrative, and/or real evidence unless your instructor indicates otherwise.

THE FINAL ASSIGNMENT

ASSIGNMENT 84: Going to Trial – The Criminal or Civil Case: *State v. Hard* or *Summers v. Hard*

Your final assignment is for you to participate as a lawyer in the trial of either the civil, *Summers v. Hard, et al.*, or the criminal case, *State v. Hard*. Your instructor will group you and others in the class into trial teams of prosecutor and defense counsel for the criminal case or plaintiff and defense attorney for the civil case. This case can be tried in one day or less or segments of the trial can be spread out over several days. Your instructor will advise you as to the schedule.

PREPARATION

Preparation for the trial entails the customary pretrial activities of developing a case theory and theme, witness preparation, deciding upon the order of witnesses, preparing proposed jury instructions, writing a trial brief, arguing pretrial motions, attending pretrial conferences, and planning for all phases of trial from jury selection to closing argument.

ASSIGNMENTS

Some of the assignments that your instructor may give are as follows:

1. Pretrial written and drafting activities, which your instructor may assign, include:

- Writing proposed jury instructions;
- Writing a trial brief; and
- Creating a demonstrative exhibit.

2. Going to trial. Your instructor will decide whether the trial will be conducted either at the courthouse and presided over by an actual trial judge or in another fashion. Detailed written directions for the performance of the trial will be provided by your instructor.

Appendix A: Checklists for Trial Skills

These checklists correspond to the chapters in *Trial Advocacy: Planning, Analysis and Strategy* (2d ed.) referred to throughout the Assignments as the *Trial Advocacy* text.

Chapter 2. Trial Persuasion Principles

Premier Trial Persuasion Principles

- ❑ Develop a persuasive message—see Chapter 3, Case Theory and Theme Development.
- ❑ Be a persuasive messenger—the successful communicator in trial.
- ❑ Use persuasive media to make your story, argument, and self dynamic in trial.

Persuasive Messenger

- ❑ To be a great communicator in trial, be sincere and project that sincerity.
- ❑ Eight points to project sincerity are these:
    - ✓ Demonstrate sincerity in voice and body language.
    - ✓ Deliver on promises.
    - ✓ Admit weaknesses.
    - ✓ Be courteous.
    - ✓ Be open.
    - ✓ Sell with plain language and integrity.

✓ Be yourself.

✓ Maintain and project a good reputation.

❑ To be a great communicator in trial, have an inspirational role model.

Persuasive Media

❑ To make your story, your argument, and yourself dynamic, use persuasive media, as follows.

❑ Non-verbal media—lawyer appearance:

✓ Dress professionally; do not let your appearance become a distraction or issue in the case.

✓ Make eye contact.

✓ Position your witnesses and yourself for greatest impact on the jury.

✓ Avoid distracting behavior, such as pacing.

✓ Manage nerves.

❑ Visual media—take full advantage of trial visuals and trial technology.

❑ Verbal media—pick persuasive language. Select powerful language that will persuade the jury.

Ethical Concern

❑ Seek to create a positive image for yourself and other trial lawyers through professional conduct and civility both in and out of court.

Chapter 3. Case Theory and Theme Development

Developing a Case Theory

1. Guide to Trial Activities

The case theory is a comprehensive guide to all aspects of trial:

❑ *Trial Preparation:* Prepare the law and facts for trial, where you will present them to support your case theory and undercut the other side's.

❑ *Trial Motions Advocacy:* Motions commonly obtain information helpful to your case theory or keep out evidence helpful to your opponent.

❑ *Objections:* Objections are designed to exclude evidence harmful to the case theory.

❑ *Jury Selection:* In the exchange with prospective jurors, you determine whether they are likely to be receptive to your case theory.

❑ *Opening Statement:* Opening statement relates the persuasive factual story component of the case theory to the jury.

❑ *Direct Examination:* Direct examinations construct the sufficient and persuasive factual story that you have promised the jury in opening statement.

❑ *Cross-Examination:* The primary purpose of cross-examination is to gain concessions that bolster the case theory. Only secondarily should cross be used to impeach the witness.

❑ *Jury Instructions:* Jury instructions are expressions of the trial lawyer's legal theory component of the case theory.

❑ *Closing Argument:* In closing argument, the trial lawyer persuades the jury of the case theory. The lawyer argues how the jury is to apply the law (counsel's legal theory) to the facts (counsel's factual theory), and thereby reach the desired verdict.

2. Ethical Considerations

Witnesses should not be coached into giving false or misleading evidence, nor should evidence be misused or destroyed.

Developing Plaintiff's Case Theory

Legal Theory

❑ *Civil Plaintiff:* Assert that each element of the claim and damages can be proven by a preponderance of the evidence.

❑ *Prosecution Legal Theory:* Alleges that every element of the crime can be proven beyond a reasonable doubt.

❑ *Selecting a Legal Theory:* Apply a two-step process in selecting a legal theory.

1. Research to identify all possible legal theories that may apply to the case.

2. Assess the strengths and weaknesses of each potential legal theory considering the legal theory

   ✓ in the abstract,

   ✓ in relation to other potential theories, and

   ✓ in conjunction with the available and potential evidence in the case.

Factual Theory

❑ Appreciate that a good factual theory is both *factually sufficient* (it is sufficient to support the plaintiff's legal theory) and *factually persuasive* (it will convince the fact finder—jury or, in a bench trial, the judge—to render the verdict that the plaintiff is seeking).

Factual Sufficiency

❑ Identify all the elements of the civil complaint or criminal charge.
❑ Present sufficient evidence on each element to establish a prima facie case.

Persuasive Story

❑ A persuasive story is a factual story that will convince the fact finder. It contains the following six essential elements:
  1. It is about *human values* (for example, family, freedom, or fairness) that the jurors believe in.
  2. It is about the loss of *human needs* (for example, safety or love).
  3. It is about *human beings* who are brought to life by the evidence and who the jurors can care about.
  4. It is *believable* and *understandable* in that it is clear and comports with stories that the jurors are familiar with. It makes sense to the jurors.
  5. It is supported by a sufficient *quantity* of evidence so that the elements are proven in accordance with the burden of proof.
  6. It is supported by a sufficient *quality* of evidence (such as credible witnesses who support the story).

Developing Defendant's Case Theory

Three Types of Defense Case Theories

❑ Attack the weaknesses in the plaintiff's case theory by:
  ✓ Attacking its *legality,*
  ✓ Attacking its *factual* sufficiency,
  ✓ Attacking its *persuasive* sufficiency, or
  ✓ Attacking its *procedural* sufficiency.
❑ Raise an affirmative defense.
❑ Negotiate.

Legal Sufficiency of Plaintiff's Case Theory

❏ Show that the plaintiff's legal theory is not valid under existing law (it's unconstitutional).

❏ Note that a fine line exists between legal and factual insufficiency.

Factual Sufficiency of Plaintiff's Case Theory

❏ Assert to the court that the plaintiff has not proven one or more elements with sufficient evidence to establish a prima facie case, so the case should not be submitted to the jury.

Persuasive Sufficiency of Plaintiff's Case

❏ Blunt or terminate the plaintiff's attempt to tell a human story about human values by:

✓ Keeping out as much as possible of the plaintiff's evidence from which that story could be told (motion in limine to exclude evidence),

✓ Telling a competing human story with human values, and/or

✓ Attacking deficiencies in quality, quantity, and plausibility of the plaintiff's case by using the perfect plaintiff's case approach.

✓ Assert to the jury that the plaintiff has not proven one or more elements of the complaint by a preponderance of the evidence in a civil case or beyond a reasonable doubt in a criminal case.

Procedural Insufficiency

Attack the procedural aspects of the plaintiff's case theory (the statute of limitations has passed, improper venue, and so on).

Affirmative Defense

Raise an independent claim, an affirmative defense, that will either mitigate or preclude a plaintiff's verdict.

Case Theory Standards for Plaintiff and Defendant

Case Assessment

Use the Case Assessment brainstorming exercise to identify case strengths and weaknesses, particularly the values that will appeal to the jury.

Multiple Legal Theories

There are three situations in which a party may want to offer more than one legal theory:

- ❏ During the early *evidence-gathering* stage before focus has narrowed to a limited number of legal theories,
- ❏ When the theories are used in *strategic sequence* (move to dismiss for insufficient evidence and, failing that, argue that the plaintiff has not met the burden of proof), and
- ❏ When *alternate* theories exist (prosecutor charges murder in the first degree but argues the lesser included crime of murder in the second degree).

Developing a Case Theme

Have a theme that meets these requirements:

- ❏ Is short—a phrase, sentence, analogy;
- ❏ Captures the essence of the case theory;
- ❏ Is memorable;
- ❏ Conveys values that the jury cares about; and
- ❏ Is suitable to the case and the fact finder.

Chapter 4. Trial Motion Advocacy

Motion Theory and Theme

- ❏ Appreciate the objective of the motion (control the information, control the outcome, control the procedure, or control the participants).
- ❏ Have a motion legal theory (MLT) to achieve the objective of the motion.
- ❏ As the responding party, have a MLT that:
  - ✓ Attacks the moving party's MLT,
  - ✓ Attacks the moving party's MFT (motion factual theory), or
  - ✓ Provides an affirmative defense to the motion.
- ❏ Have a motion factual theory (MFT) that is both:
  - ✓ Sufficient, in that it supports the MLT, and
  - ✓ Persuasive because it makes sense, is logical, reveals values that the judge will hold (linking the values to the rationale behind the MLT), and is a human story.

❑ Have a motion theme, that is, a short statement that encapsulates the motion theory—particularly the MLT—and expresses values that will appeal to the motion's judge.

Making a Factual Record

❑ Determine whether the motion requires a factual record and, if such a record is required, who has the burden of making the record.

❑ In making a *documentary factual record* (affidavit, discovery response, deposition excerpts, exhibits), ensure that there is a sufficient factual record supporting the motion and that the documents are authenticated and otherwise satisfy the evidentiary rules.

❑ When presenting evidence at an *evidentiary hearing,* create a factual record, using the skills and techniques covered in Chapter 8, Exhibits and the Visual Trial, and in Chapter 9, Direct Examination: Building the Case.

Getting a Hearing on the Motion

❑ Properly serve the motion on opposing counsel.

❑ Confer with opposing counsel regarding the motion and prepare a certificate of the conference if such a certificate is required.

❑ Think about the strategies of requesting a single hearing or separate hearings.

❑ Obtain a hearing time and date and serve a notice of the motion.

The Written Motion or Response

❑ Make sure the motion has all the essential supporting components:
  - ✓ Notice of motion;
  - ✓ Memorandum of law with the appropriate subsections (statement of the case, request for relief, statement of facts, statement of issues, argument, and conclusion);
  - ✓ Attachments;
  - ✓ Proposed order; and
  - ✓ Proof of service.

❑ Make sure the response to the motion has the essential elements—the memorandum of law, attachments, proposed order, proof of service.

❑ Write a persuasive story in the statement of facts:
  - ✓ Tell a story about human values that will appeal to the motion's judge and demonstrates a human story.

✓ Use storytelling devices, such as beginning in a way that will capture the judge's attention.

❑ Frame the issues so that the question suggests the conclusion that you want the court to reach and set out the facts that support your position.

❑ In the argument section of the memorandum of law:

✓ Try to employ the three types of Aristotelian arguments—appeals to logic, appeals to ethics, and appeals to emotion; and

✓ Follow the syllogistic structure of argument (state the law, apply it to the facts, and state the conclusion).

❑ Throughout the motion and memorandum of law, repeat the motion theme and rephrase it so that it remains fresh.

❑ Take advantage of effective writing styles and structures:

✓ Making all writing accurate,

✓ Using clarity of expression,

✓ Avoiding hyperbole,

✓ Avoiding personal attacks,

✓ Properly citing legal authority,

✓ Citing and dealing with contrary controlling legal authority,

✓ Carefully proofreading for errors and misspellings, and

✓ Submitting the document within court's deadline.

Oral Argument on the Motion or Response

❑ Begin by

✓ Preparing for this part of the argument by writing it out and practicing it,

✓ Introducing yourself and who you represent,

✓ Asking to reserve time for rebuttal if you are the moving party,

✓ Capturing the judge's attention,

✓ Getting to the essence of your motion or response by telling the judge what you want, and

✓ Stating your theme.

❑ The middle—making the arguments:

✓ Organize the arguments so you lead with your strongest argument.

✓ Make a factual argument that tells a human story, one about human values that underpin the rationale behind the advocate's MLT.

    ✓ Present the legal argument in the syllogistic structure; rely on controlling statutory, case law, or other authority; and avoid string citing.

❑ Conclude with your theme and a request for what you want (request to grant or deny the motion). As with your beginning, write this part out and practice it over and over until you can deliver it smoothly and naturally. Finally, when you have said what you have to say, sit down.

❑ Know the judge by scouting.

❑ Field the judge's questions effectively by adhering to these techniques:

    ✓ Prepare for questions by brainstorming to determine what the tough questions will be and planning answers to them.

    ✓ Watch to see how the argument is being received and adjust if needed.

    ✓ Stop if the judge speaks and do not interrupt.

    ✓ Listen carefully to the judge's question.

    ✓ Pause before answering and organize your thoughts.

    ✓ Answer the question and do not say it will be answered later.

    ✓ Maintain composure—the best remedy for nervousness is hard work preparing and practicing.

    ✓ Be candid with the court—saying that you don't know is all right.

    ✓ Engage in a dialogue with the motion's judge; welcome the exchange.

❑ Be thoroughly prepared on the facts and law.

❑ When permitted and appropriate, use visuals to enhance the argument.

❑ Show courtesy and respect to everyone in the court system—judge, lower bench, and opposing counsel (never engage in personal attacks on opposing counsel).

❑ Find the right courtroom position—behind a podium only if required; stand up at the bar if permitted; and, most of all, find the position that enhances your communication with the motion's judge.

❑ Dress and groom professionally.

❑ Use appropriate body language:

    ✓ Avoid distracting habits (tapping the pen).

    ✓ Avoid reading and maintain good eye contact by having a minimal amount of paper at hand—use the folder technique.

    ✓ Make appropriate hand gestures.

❑ Apply good speech techniques:

    ✓ Use a clear voice.

✓ Modulate your voice.

✓ Pause, particularly between arguments.

✓ Watch out for repeated placeholders and verbal hiccups—*you know, umm,* and the like.

✓ Take advantage of speech devices to keep your presentation interesting (analogies, rhetorical questions, similes, and so on).

Reacting to an Adverse Ruling on the Motion

❑ Determine whether there is authority authorizing an appeal of the ruling.

❑ Exercise common sense in deciding whether to appeal:

✓ Determine if the appellate court is likely to reverse.

✓ Decide whether it is worth the time and expense.

✓ Decide if there are other unfavorable consequences of an appeal.

Ethical Considerations

❑ Offer adverse controlling legal authority and, if possible, distinguish it.

❑ Do not bring a frivolous motion.

❑ Use the motion only for an appropriate purpose.

Chapter 5. Making and Meeting Objections

Making Objections

Purpose

The objection is intended to accomplish a purpose, such as:

❑ Controlling the information to the jury (exclude evidence),

❑ Controlling opposing counsel from alluding to inadmissible evidence, or

❑ Preserving error for appeal.

Judgment

Counsel exercises judgment in objecting, ensuring that:

❑ The objection is made on solid legal and factual grounds,

❑ The objection is consistent with counsel's case theory, and

❑ The objection considers the audience—judge and jury (counsel does not appear to be making frivolous objections).

Trial Strategies

❑ The objection is timely made, shielding the jury from inadmissible evidence.

❑ The objection is stated appropriately either in the preferred, technical, or understandable phrasing, depending on the situation.

❑ The objection is coupled with a request for a special remedy if one is needed (for example, strike the testimony).

❑ When the objection is designed to protect the record, counsel:

   ✓ Makes sure that the record exists,

   ✓ States specific grounds for the objection, and

   ✓ Requests a limiting instruction if necessary.

❑ Counsel's demeanor, tone of voice, and behavior are proper (for example, counsel does not engage in banter with opposing counsel).

❑ Counsel requests a sidebar or to have the jury excused when argument or evidence should not be heard by the jury.

❑ Counsel combats improper behavior of opposing counsel.

Meeting Objections

Preparation

❑ Counsel is prepared to meet the objection with factual and legal arguments.

❑ Counsel has prepared a pocket brief for major issues.

Silence or Phrasing

❑ Counsel remains silent, awaiting the court's ruling, when no response is necessary.

❑ Counsel's response to the objection succinctly states the legal response, unless the court calls for more.

Trial Strategies

❑ Counsel protects the record by making sure there is one.

❑ Counsel makes an offer of proof when evidence is excluded, unless the evidence is evident from the context.

❑ Counsel requests a limiting instruction if necessary.

❑ Counsel's demeanor, tone of voice, and behavior are proper (for example, counsel does not engage in banter with opposing counsel).

❑ Counsel requests a sidebar or to have the jury excused when argument or evidence should not be heard by the jury.

Ethical Boundaries—Making and Meeting Objections

In objecting or responding, counsel does not:

❑ State an improper personal opinion,

❑ Mention any matter that is not supported by admissible evidence,

❑ Inject irrelevant information, or

❑ Engage in conduct that causes an unwarranted delay in the proceedings.

Chapter 6. Jury Selection: Two-Way Exchange

Understanding of the Procedure

Counsel understood the jury selection process:

❑ The order of questioning,

❑ Types of questions,

❑ The grounds for a for-cause challenge and how to exercise it,

❑ How to rehabilitate a prospective juror challenged for cause, and

❑ How to exercise peremptory challenges, including:

    ✓ *Batson* challenge and requirements,

    ✓ Mechanics of exercising peremptories, and

    ✓ The number allotted.

Organization

Counsel was organized and used a:

    ✓ Jury selection binder,

    ✓ Juror seating chart,

     ✓ Challenges chart,

     ✓ Case summary sheet, and

     ✓ List of witnesses.

Building a Positive Relationship with the Jurors

Counsel developed a positive relationship by

     ❑ Projecting honesty and sincerity,

     ❑ Carrying on a conversation with the prospective jurors by:

        ✓ Asking open-ended and close-end questions where appropriate,

        ✓ Speaking so the questions were easily understood,

        ✓ Using a conversational and friendly tone,

        ✓ Listening attentively,

        ✓ Managing the discussion, and

        ✓ Remaining nonjudgmental.

Questioning

     ❑ Lawyer used introductory remarks to relax the jurors and give them a snapshot of the case.

     ❑ Lawyer used concluding questions and, if permitted, closing remarks.

     ❑ Questions were designed to elicit information that would aid in exercising challenges and cause the jurors to be receptive to the case theory.

     ❑ Questions covered these areas:

        ✓ Challenge for cause areas,

        ✓ Case weaknesses,

        ✓ Advancement of the case theory and theme,

        ✓ Trial questions (burden of proof), and

        ✓ Case issues (damages).

Exercising Challenges

     ❑ Challenges were exercised against prospective jurors who probably would not reach the desired verdict.

Ethical Considerations

     ❑ Counsel did not make an extrajudicial media statement likely to prejudice the trial or other proceeding.

❑ In a criminal case, the prosecutor took reasonable steps to prevent law enforcement and others associated with the prosecution from making statements that the prosecutor would be prohibited from making.

❑ Counsel did not try to influence a prospective juror or juror by means prohibited by law and, after discharge of the jury, did not communicate with the juror when the juror indicated a wish not to communicate, when prohibited by law or the court or when the communication involved misrepresentation, coercion, duress, or harassment.

Chapter 7. Opening Statement: Storytelling

Content

The opening statement:

❑ Concisely states the legal theory without arguing or invading the judge's prerogative to instruct on the law;

❑ Includes sufficient facts to support the legal theory;

❑ Incorporates the essentials of a persuasive story:
  - ✓ Human values,
  - ✓ Human needs,
  - ✓ Human story—usually about the client,
  - ✓ Believable and understandable story,
  - ✓ Quantity of evidence described is compelling, and
  - ✓ Quality of evidence is convincing.

❑ Is a statement of fact, not argument;

❑ Is not too detailed;

❑ Covers only admissible evidence that counsel expects to prove;

❑ Candidly addresses case weaknesses;

❑ Anticipates and refutes the other side's case theory when permissible (prosecutor may not attempt to shift the burden to the defense); and

❑ Has a well-crafted case theme.

Structure

❑ The opening statement begins with an attention-getter (theme, dramatic setting of the scene).

❑ The body of the opening flows smoothly and tells the story with a clear and understandable structure (flashback, chronological).

❑ The opening statement concludes by referring back to the theme and reasons for the requested verdict.

Storytelling, Staging, and Delivery

❑ Counsel projects sincerity.

❑ Counsel avoids distracting behavior (pacing back and forth).

❑ Counsel uses eye contact with jurors.

❑ Counsel does not read the opening.

❑ Counsel uses effective storytelling techniques, such as:

    ✓ Choosing persuasive language,

    ✓ Eliminating legal terms and legalese,

    ✓ Employing words with connotations,

    ✓ Adopting a point of view, such as the client's,

    ✓ Shifting to present tense for effect, and

    ✓ Pacing at an appropriate rate (slowed when covering dramatic facts).

❑ Opening is of appropriate length of time.

❑ The opening is staged successfully:

    ✓ Counsel positions her body to hold the jury's attention.

    ✓ Counsel makes purposeful movements.

❑ The opening uses trial visuals effectively:

    ✓ Counsel ensures use is permissible.

    ✓ Visual is persuasive.

    ✓ Counsel positions equipment and visuals appropriately.

    ✓ Counsel has a backup plan if equipment malfunctions.

Ethical Boundaries

❑ Counsel does not state a personal opinion.

❑ Counsel does not overpromise something that cannot be proved.

❑ Counsel does not introduce irrelevant matter.

Chapter 8. Exhibits and the Visual Trial

Planning to Use Exhibits

❑ Identify exhibits in existence and collect and preserve them:

✓ Determine if other exhibits and trial visuals are called for and create them.

✓ Incorporate the essentials of a persuasive story:

✦ Human values,

✦ Human needs,

✦ Human story—usually about the client,

✦ Believable and understandable story,

✦ Quantity of evidence described is compelling, and

✦ Quality of evidence is convincing.

✓ Conduct legal research and move in limine to admit the exhibit or prepare a trial brief if needed.

✓ Plan to establish the foundation for admissibility of the exhibit.

✓ Prepare your witnesses to work with exhibits in trial (show them the exhibits and rehearse).

✓ Have an exhibit list and have the exhibits premarked if possible.

❑ Introduce an exhibit:

✓ Have the clerk mark the exhibit if it is not premarked.

✓ Show the exhibit to opposing counsel.

✓ Establish the evidentiary foundation for the exhibit.

✓ Offer the exhibit and meet any objections to it.

✓ Make a record.

❑ Display the exhibit:

✓ Scout the courtroom to determine what equipment is available.

✓ Gain permission from the judge to bring in and use equipment for displaying exhibits, such as a document camera.

✓ Make arrangements to bring equipment to court.

✓ Determine how to display the exhibit with these alternatives, among others:

Document camera;

Publishing or parading the exhibit;

Showing the exhibit or reading a documentary exhibit;

Placing the exhibit, such as a diagram, on an easel; or

Projecting the computer image on a screen or monitor.

❑ Display the proper demeanor and behavior when working with exhibits.

❑ Time the introduction of the exhibit so it has impact on the jury.

Essential Evidence Rules

❑ Adhere to the four-step approach and ask yourself the following questions:

  ✓ Is the exhibit relevant?

  ✓ Is the exhibit authenticated or identified?

  ✓ Is the exhibit proper under Federal Rule of Evidence 403?

  ✓ Is the exhibit otherwise admissible?

Software and Trial Presentations

❑ Computer software, such as PowerPoint, can be used to create and display visuals.

❑ Have a backup plan (run off computer slides on letter-sized paper so they can be displayed with the document camera).

❑ A trial visuals consulting business not only can create the trial visuals but also can appear in court as trial support to display the visual.

❑ Obtain court permission to display trial visuals.

Ethical Considerations

❑ Do not obstruct opposing party's access to exhibits.

❑ Do not display an exhibit to the jury before the court has ruled on its admissibility or it is otherwise permissible to do so, such as during opening statement.

Chapter 9. Direct Examination: Building the Case

Content

The attorney conducting the direct:

❑ Advances the case theory;

❑ Elicits evidence that supports elements of the legal theory (claim or defense or counterclaim);

❑ Delivers a compelling story by concentrating on the six essentials of a persuasive factual story:

✓ Human values that the jury cares about (fairness),

✓ Human needs (personal safety),

✓ Human story (facts that will sway the jury to care about the client),

✓ Believable and understandable story (makes common sense),

✓ Quantity of evidence (the facts testified to by the witness contributes to the evidence required to meet the burden of proof), and

✓ Quality of evidence (the facts elicited show that the witness is credible).

❑ Where appropriate, reveals case weaknesses to inoculate the jury; and

❑ Seeks to elicit admissible evidence under applicable evidence law.

Structure

❑ Introductory questions accomplish these objectives:

✓ Get the jurors' attention (start with the first question that is likely on the jurors' minds).

✓ Accredit the witness.

✓ Put the witness at ease and introduce the witness to the jurors.

❑ The body of the direct is readily understandable by the jury because it uses one or more organizational structures:

✓ Chronological,

✓ By subject area,

✓ By legal elements,

✓ Straight narrative.

❑ The conclusion of direct and any redirect are on a high note.

Essential Evidence Rules

❑ The witness is competent.

❑ The witness has personal knowledge.

❑ Counsel impeaches his own witness if need be.

❑ Counsel does not ask leading questions unless on preliminary matters, uncontested matters, or where they are addressed to a hostile witness or adverse party.

❑ Direct delves only into relevant material.

Conducting a Successful Direct

❑ The witness is well prepared to testify.

❑ Counsel is positioned in the courtroom so the witness is the center of attention and enabled to communicate directly to the jury.

❑ Language from crucial jury instructions is incorporated into the questioning.

❑ The form of each question is designed to facilitate communication and make the testimony flow smoothly. Each question:

✓ Is brief and simple,

✓ Is understandable (open-ended for well-prepared and articulate witnesses),

✓ Omits negatives,

✓ Complies with evidence rules, and

✓ Does not include follow-up affirmations by counsel (*Okay*).

❑ Counsel listens to the witness's answer and responds accordingly (asks follow-up questions to clarify an answer).

❑ Direct highlights important information using techniques such as:

✓ Looping,

✓ Using exhibits and courtroom demonstrations, and

✓ Stop-action.

❑ Direct maintains the jury's interest with trial techniques such as:

✓ Maintaining energy in asking questions, listening, and responding;

✓ Varying voice volume and tone, form of the question, positioning in the courtroom, and so on; and

✓ Conducting a rehearsed courtroom demonstration and working with exhibits so as to break up the testimony and maintain jurors' interest.

Exhibits

❑ Direct examination introduces exhibits necessary to prove the case theory.

❑ Exhibits are used persuasively.

Problematic Witnesses

❑ Direct takes the witness's special problems into account (elicits testimony from a very young child to show the witness is competent and treats the witness gently).

Visual Trial

❑ Direct employs visuals to make the direct persuasive and understandable.

Appellate Record

❑ Counsel makes a record for appeal.

Redirect

❑ Successfully undercuts damage done by cross-examination.
❑ Ends on a high note.

Order of Proof

❑ The order in which the witnesses are called in the case-in-chief is the most effective way of convincingly communicating the case theory.

Ethical Boundaries

❑ The examination does not offer evidence that counsel knows to be false.
❑ Counsel remedies the situation if the witness introduces false evidence.

Chapter 10. Cross-Examination: Concession Seeking

Content

❑ Cross-examination serves the primary purpose of advancing counsel's case theory or undercutting the other side's case theory.
❑ The cross seeks concessions supporting counsel's case theory or undercutting the other side's.
❑ Cross-examination serves the secondary purpose of impeachment.
❑ Counsel's impeachment cross explores one of the nine principal areas of impeachment:
    1. Improbability,
    2. Prior inconsistent statement,
    3. Prior convictions,

4. Lack of personal knowledge,

5. Mental and sensory deficiencies,

6. Bias and interest,

7. Prior bad acts probative on untruthfulness,

8. Contradiction, and

9. Character witness ("Have you heard . . . ?")

Construction

❑ Cross flows smoothly and is understandable.

❑ Questions are framed appropriately: almost always leading, sometimes anticipatory or accusatory under special circumstances, and seldom, if ever, interrogatory.

❑ Questions are short and comprehensible.

❑ The cross is sequenced effectively, using this order:

1. Concessions first,

2. Topical and/or chronological, and

3. Finishing on a high note.

❑ Transitions are labeled clearly ("Now let's talk about . . .").

Character

❑ Cross-examiner comes across as a sincere seeker of truth who shows courtesy and professionalism toward the witness.

Control

❑ Counsel controls the witness using Irving Younger's Ten Commandments and varies the approach only when counsel has good reason to do so:

1. Be brief.

2. Use plain words and short questions.

3. Leading questions only.

4. Be prepared—know the answer.

5. Listen to the answer.

6. Don't quarrel with the witness.

7. Don't ask the witness for an explanation.

8. Don't repeat the direct examination.

9. Limit examination—avoid too many questions.

10. Persuade during closing not cross-examination.

❑ Counsel uses control techniques:
  ✓ Secure an agreement.
  ✓ Repeat the question.
  ✓ Ask the witness to repeat the question.
  ✓ Become more confrontational.
  ✓ Palm-toward-witness stop gesture.

Essential Evidence Rules

❑ Counsel asks leading questions.
❑ Counsel abides by evidentiary law applicable to these areas of impeachment:
  ✓ Improbability, bias, motive, perception, and ability to relate;
  ✓ Prior inconsistent statements;
  ✓ Prior convictions; and
  ✓ Prior bad acts probative of untruthfulness.

Strategies

❑ No cross when it serves no purpose.
❑ Counsel's position in the courtroom directs the jury's attention to counsel and allows counsel to observe and have an effect on the witness.
❑ Counsel's demeanor toward the witness is that of a sincere seeker of truth who is courteous to the witness but does not tolerate witness deception or evasion.
❑ Counsel seldom reads from notes and infrequently takes notes.
❑ Counsel highlights important aspects of the testimony by using the following techniques:
  ✓ Looping,
  ✓ Exhibits and demonstrations,
  ✓ Silence, and
  ✓ Writing the answer so the jury can see it.

Visuals

❑ Uses visuals during cross.

Ethical Boundaries

❑ Counsel does not allude to matter that trial counsel cannot reasonably believe is relevant or that won't be supported by admissible evidence.

Chapter 11. Experts: Yours and Theirs

Expert Direct Examination

Content

❑ The direct examination of the expert advances the case theory
❑ The direct examination elicits evidence that supports elements of the legal theory (claim or defense or counterclaim).

Components of an Expert's Direct Examination

The direct effectively covered these five components:

❑ The expert's qualifications;
❑ Reliability of the field of expertise;
❑ Factual basis supporting the expert's opinion;
❑ Countering the other side's attack; and
❑ The expert's opinions.

Conducting the Direct

Counsel did the following:

❑ Put the expert center stage and enabled the expert to teach the jury (assuming a good expert);
❑ Had the expert testify in understandable terms and when necessary sought translations of technical terminology;
❑ Provided the expert with exhibits and technology that allowed the expert to visually explain findings and opinions to the jury; and
❑ Utilized storytelling techniques to make the expert's testimony understandable, interesting and persuasive.

Ethical Boundaries

❑ The direct examination does not offer evidence that counsel knows to be false

❑ Counsel remedies the situation if the witness introduces false evidence.

Excluding the Testimony

As an alternative to cross-examination, counsel makes a motion to exclude the expert's testimony.

Preparation

Counsel prepares well for the cross-examination by doing the following:

❑ Consulting with her own expert;

❑ Obtaining full discovery; and

❑ Researching and reading the expert's published work, reports, and transcripts as well as other pertinent literature in the field.

Content

❑ The cross-examination serves the primary purpose of advancing counsel's case theory or undercutting the other side's case theory.

❑ The cross seeks concessions supporting counsel's case theory or undercutting the other side's.

❑ The cross-examination serves the secondary purpose of impeachment.

❑ Counsel's impeachment cross explores one of the fourteen areas of impeachment.

Construction

❑ Cross flows smoothly and is understandable.

❑ Questions are framed appropriately: almost always leading, sometimes anticipatory or accusatory under special circumstances, and seldom, if ever, interrogatory.

❑ Questions are short and comprehensible.

❑ The cross was sequenced effectively, using this order:

  ✓ Concessions first,

  ✓ Topical and/or chronological, and

  ✓ Finishing on a high note.

❑ Transitions are labeled clearly ("Now let's talk about . . .").

Character

❑ Cross-examiner comes across as a sincere seeker of truth who shows courtesy and professionalism toward the witness.

Control

❑ Counsel controls the witness using Irving Younger's Ten Commandments and varies the approach only when counsel has good reason to do so:

1. Be brief.
2. Use plain words and short questions.
3. Leading questions only.
4. Be prepared—know the answer.
5. Listen to the answer.
6. Don't quarrel with the witness.
7. Don't ask the witness for an explanation.
8. Don't repeat the direct examination.
9. Limit examination—avoid too many questions.
10. Persuade during closing, not cross-examination.

❑ Counsel uses control techniques:

✓ Secure an agreement.
✓ Repeat the question.
✓ Ask the witness to repeat the question.
✓ Become more confrontational.
✓ Palm-toward-witness stop gesture.

Impeachment

❑ Counsel successfully impeaches the witness and/or witness's testimony.

✓ Expert witness areas:
1. Qualifications,
2. Reliability of the field,
3. Basis for opinion,
4. Opinion, and
5. Learned treatises.

Ethical Concerns

☐ Counsel does not allude to matter that trial counsel cannot reasonably believe is relevant or that won't be supported by admissible evidence.

Chapter 12. Jury Instructions: The Jury's Law

Drafting and Organizing Proposed Instructions

☐ Adopt pattern jury instructions or modifications of them when possible,

☐ Be written in plain English,

☐ Embody counsel's legal theory,

☐ Be balanced expressions of the law,

☐ Be organized in a logical sequence,

☐ Correctly state the law,

☐ Reflect the evidence presented at trial, and

☐ Properly influence how the jury is to make factual determinations.

Presenting and Advocating for Instructions

☐ The proposed instructions are in the proper form.

☐ Counsel advocates for proposed instructions during counsels' conference with the trial judge.

☐ Counsel properly offers alternative proposed instructions or withdraws proposed instructions when necessary.

☐ Counsel effectively argues and takes exception to instructions during the hearing on instructions.

☐ Counsel pays close attention during the reading of instructions and takes remedial steps if a problem arises.

Ethical Considerations

Counsel advocates for a correct statement of the law in the instructions.

Chapter 13. Closing Arguments: Art of Argument

Preparation

- ❑ Preparation begins soon after entry into the case, and counsel starts keeping notes of ideas for closing.
- ❑ Prior to trial, closing argument is written out, with final editing to be done during trial, and closing is reduced to outline notes.
- ❑ Rehearses closing argument and commits opening and concluding remarks to memory so they will flow smoothly.

Content

- ❑ Case theories serve as guides for planning closing.
- ❑ Regarding the legal theories, these jury instructions, among others, serve as the core around which to craft closing argument:
  - ✓ Elements of the claim or defense,
  - ✓ Burden of proof,
  - ✓ Issues in dispute, and
  - ✓ The other side's case theory.
- ❑ In arguing the factual theory, counsel uses jury instructions that pertain to crucial facts as well a story embodying those facts.
- ❑ The case theme is incorporated into the closing.
- ❑ Closing meets the other side's case theory and attacks.
- ❑ Juror beliefs and expectations that could be detrimental to the case are identified, met, or distinguished from the case on trial.

Length

- ❑ Length of closing is suitable to the complexity of the case, and counsel does not run overly long.

Aristotelian Appeals

- ❑ Closing makes all three appeals: logical, emotional, and ethical.
- ❑ Persuasive language is used, including:
  - ✓ Words with connotations; and
  - ✓ Rhetorical devices, such as postponement, concession, antithesis, metaphors, similes, analogies, and rhetorical questions.

Structure

❑ The closing begins by seizing the jury's attention.

❑ The body of the closing is well organized and emphasizes the strengths of the case before dealing with case weaknesses or the other side's attack.

❑ The closing concludes by referring back to the theme and reasons for the requested verdict, thus motivating the jury to make the right decision.

❑ Rebuttal refutes the other side's arguments and finishes strong.

Delivery

❑ Counsel does the following:

✓ Projects sincerity;

✓ Avoids distracting behavior, such as pacing back and forth;

✓ Maintains eye contact with jurors;

✓ Does not read the closing;

✓ Positions his body to hold the jury's attention; and

✓ Makes purposeful movements.

❑ Counsel uses trial visuals effectively:

✓ Ensures use is permissible,

✓ Makes visuals persuasive,

✓ Positions equipment and visuals appropriately, and

✓ Has a backup plan if equipment malfunctions.

Ethical Boundaries

❑ Counsel does not state a personal opinion.

❑ Counsel does not venture outside the record.

❑ Counsel does not introduce irrelevant matter.

❑ Counsel does not invoke the golden rule.

Appendix B: Trial Case File Table of Contents

CRIMINAL CASE FILE: *STATE v. HARD*

Media Information

      Entry 1.   Excerpts from Newspaper Articles

      Entry 2.   Television and Radio Log

Pleadings

      Entry 3.   Information

Police Reports

      Entry 4.   Ruston Police Department Report by Detective Tharp

                  Suspect Information

                  Follow-up Police Report

                  Witness List

                  Evidence List

Documents, Letters, and Reports

      Entry 5.   Alcohol Influence Report

      Entry 6.   Application to Transfer Pistol

                  Copy of Ed Hard's Check

                  Department of the Treasury Firearms Transaction Record

      Entry 7.   Letter, Medical Examiner Autopsy Report, and Toxicology Report

      Entry 8.   Death Certificate

      Entry 9.   Dental Record of Ed Hard

      Entry 10. FBI Criminal Records

      Entry 11. Judgments and Sentences for Edward Hard

      Entry 12. Letter and Hospital Records of Bruno Summers

Entry 13. Neo-Nazi Survivalist Organization Card (Enlarged)

Entry 14. Crime Laboratory Report

Statements Taken by Ruston Police Department

Entry 15. Peter Dean

Entry 16. Thomas Donaldson

Entry 17. Edward Hard

Entry 18. Bert Kain

Entry 19. Roberta Montbank

Entry 20. Cindy Rigg

Entry 21. Deborah Summers

Entry 22. Officer F. West

Entry 23. Officer M. Yale

Statements Taken by Defendant Hard's Attorney

Entry 24. John Gooding

Entry 25. Rebecca Karr

Curriculum Vitae

Entry 26. Dr. Brett Day, Attending Doctor

Entry 27. Dr. L.R. Jackson, Medical Examiner

Entry 28. H. Tredwell, Firearms Examiner

Diagrams

Entry 29. Scale Diagram, Garage Tavern

Entry 30. Scale Diagram, Gull Gas Station

Entry 31. Diagram (Not to Scale) Edward Hard's House

Photographs

Entry 32. Garage Tavern Exterior Photos (A-C)
Garage Tavern Interiors Photos (D-Q)

Entry 33. Photographs After Shooting of Bruno Summers, September 3, 20XX (Photo A and Photo B)

Entry 34. Family Photographs of Bruno, Deborah, and the Summers Children (Photos A-J)

Entry 35. Gun and Bullets (Photo A and Photo B)

Entry 36. Knife (Photo)

CIVIL CASE FILE: *SUMMERS v. HARD* (INCLUDES CRIMINAL TRIAL CASE FILE, ENTRIES 1-36)

Pleadings

Entry 37.   Summons

Entry 38.   Complaint (for critique only)

Answers (for critique only):

Entry 39.   Ed Hard

Entry 40.   Davola, Donaldson, and Apple

Documents

Bills

Entry 41.   AAB Ambulance Bill

Entry 42.   Holiday View Funeral Parlor Bill

Entry 43.   Mercy Hospital Bill

Deborah Summers's Juvenile Court and Medical Records:

Entry 44.   Jamner County Health Department

Entry 45.   Neva County Medical Services

Entry 46.   Major Juvenile Court Records

Economic Reports

Entry 47.   Dr. Bruce Hann

Entry 48.   Dr. Thomas Monday

Insurance Company Policies

Entry 49.   EKKO Insurance

Entry 50.   SAPO Insurance

Psychologists Reports and Files – Emotional Distress

Entry 51.   Report and Files of Dr. Pat Gage, Doctor for Deborah Summers

Entry 52.   Supplemental Report of Dr. Pat Gage, Doctor for Ronnie Summers

Entry 53.   Report of Dr. Ennis Martinez on Deborah Summers

Entry 54.   Report of Dr. Ennis Martinez on Ronnie Summers

Tavern Management Reports

Entry 55.   Dr. Dale Thompson

Entry 56.   Dr. Ben Kaplan

Entry 57.   Letter to Roberta Montbank from Plaintiffs' Attorney

Photographs
    Entry 58.   University Fitness – Bruno Summers's Business
Curriculum Vitae
    Entry 59.   Dr. David Bowman, Psychologist
    Entry 60.   Dr. Sherman Croup, Doctor for Deborah Summers
    Entry 61.   Dr. Pat Gage
    Entry 62.   Dr. Bruce D. Hann, Economist
    Entry 63.   Dr. Hollis Lufkin, Psychiatrist
    Entry 64.   Dr. Ennis Martinez
    Entry 65.   Dr. Thomas Monday, Economist
    Entry 66.   Dr. Edward Risseen, Doctor for Deborah Summers
    Entry 67.   Dr. Dale Thompson
Deposition and Interrogatories Excerpts and Statement
  Deposition Excerpts
    Entry 68.   Mary Apple
    Entry 69.   Dr. Sherman Croup
    Entry 70.   M.C. Davola
    Entry 71.   Brett Day, M.D.
    Entry 72.   Peter Dean
    Entry 73.   Fred Faye
    Entry 74.   Betty Frank, R.N.
    Entry 75.   John Gooding
    Entry 76.   Edward Hard
    Entry 77.   Bert Kain
    Entry 78.   Rebecca Karr
    Entry 79.   Hollis Lufkin, M.D.
    Entry 80.   Roberta Montbank
    Entry 81.   Edward Risseen, M.D.
    Entry 82.   Deborah Summers
    Entry 83.   Ronnie Summers
    Entry 84.   Karen Sway
    Entry 85.   Officer M. Yale
  Interrogatories
    Entry 86.   Edward Hard to Plaintiffs (Excerpt)
    Entry 87.   Deborah Summers to Edward T. Hard (Excerpt)
  Statement
    Entry 88.   Roberta Montbank Statement (EKKO Insurance Company)

GENERAL RESEARCH CASE FILE

Case History and Witnesses

    Entry 89. Case History

    Entry 90. Summary of Witness Testimony for Trial

State of Major Statutes

    Entry 91. Criminal Statutes (Excerpts)

    Entry 92. Civil Statutes (Excerpts)

State of Major Civil Administrative Regulations

    Entry 93. Excerpts

State of Major Court Rules

    Entry 94. Court Rules (Excerpts)

State of Major Rules of Evidence

    Entry 95. Evidence Rules (Excerpts)

State of Major Rules of Professional Conduct

    Entry 96. Rules of Professional Conduct (Based upon the ABA Model Rules)

State of Major Jury Instructions

    Entry 97. Criminal

    Entry 98. Civil

Medical Glossary

    Entry 99. Excerpts

Research Memoranda – Civil and Criminal

    Entry 100. Acts of Misconduct; Reputation

    Entry 101. Authentication – Handwriting, Telephone, Voice, Scientific Evidence

    Entry 102. Demonstrative Evidence

    Entry 103. Dying Declarations; Excited Utterances

    Entry 104. Habit Evidence

    Entry 105. Husband-Wife Privilege; Communication

    Entry 106. Jury Selection

    Entry 107. Lesser Included Offenses

    Entry 108. Lost or Destroyed Evidence

    Entry 109. Opening Statement

    Entry 110. Opinion – Lay and Expert

    Entry 111. Photographs

    Entry 112. Prior Convictions, Adult and Juvenile

    Entry 113. Psychiatric Testimony, Prediction of Dangerousness

Entry 114.   Subsequent Remedial Measures

Entry 115.   Use of Treatises

Entry 116.   Video and Audio Admissibility

Entry 117.   Witnesses – Testimony from a Child; Witness Competency

Entry 118.   Wrongful Death; Emotional Distress

Entry 119.   Duty to Defend

Entry 120.   Fifth Amendment

Entry 121.   Expert Witnesses; Methodological Reliability

Entry 122.   *Morgan's Evidentiary Foundations Courtroom Handbook for State of Major Trial Lawyers* (Excerpts)

Entry 123.   Visual Storytelling: A Sample Presentation in the *Summers Case.pdf*

Entry 123.   Visual Storytelling: A Sample Presentation in the *Summers Case.ppt* (PowerPoint Slide Presentation)